Penguin Books

Social Anarchism
Giovanni Baldelli

Giovanni Baldelli teaches languages at St Olave's School
in Orpington, Kent. He was born in Milan. In his early
youth he became actively involved in underground work
against the Fascist regime and, when discovered, was able
to find refuge in France. This is where he first encountered
anarchists, became one himself, and devoted his life to the
anarchist cause. He presided over the International
Anarchist Congress in London (1958) and has acted as
Secretary of the International Anarchist Commission. He
continues to write widely on numerous subjects related to
the anarchist viewpoint and, as a thinker, remains in the
forefront of the worldwide anarchist movement.

Social Anarchism

Giovanni Baldelli

Penguin Books

Penguin Books Ltd, Harmondsworth,
Middlesex, England
Penguin Books Australia Ltd,
Ringwood, Victoria, Australia

First published in the USA by Aldine 1971
Published by Penguin Books 1972
Copyright © Aldine, Atherton, Inc., 1971

Made and printed in Great Britain by
Cox & Wyman Ltd, London, Reading and Fakenham
Set in Intertype Baskerville

This book is dedicated to friendship,
to which it owes so much

Contents

Preface

What would an *ethical* society be like? What might its principles of organization be? Giovanni Baldelli's answer is that the society would be *anarchist*: without laws, without political authority, without concentrations of power.

Now, such a vision of ethical society, of a truly 'good' society, is widely acknowledged to be an unobjectionable ideal – but only *as* an ideal. Such a vision is usually dismissed as utopian and irrelevant because it is thought to depend on an overly generous view of an elusive something called 'human nature'. In most textbooks of political theory one finds no discussion of the anarchists' logically obvious alternative to the governmental systems which the books analyse and appraise. Earnest ethical writers who have tried to frame conceptions of an ideal society have usually been unable even to imagine it functioning without political authority; from Plato onwards the tradition is that the ethical society requires a strong central power. In short, these writers have doubted that 'ordinary' human beings can ever be autonomous ethical persons. The result is a picture of an ethical society – if one can without contradiction call it that – composed of human beings incapable of living ethical lives in the absence of a government that enforces the contract of peace and justice. But an ethical society composed of persons not voluntarily ethical is not only a severely limited ideal, perhaps even a contradiction in terms, but it is also a first step in justification of governments which know what is 'good for' people.

In one political tradition, to be sure, the Marxist, a stateless society is envisaged as the end-ideal. In Marx's theory, however, the ethical society requires the State for its realization. When by means of the state a classless society has been achieved (it is said) the State will progressively lose importance and will 'wither away'. But this remote event, although plainly indicated by Marx's dialectical analysis, enters in no practical way into the thinking of Marx's followers, and from Marx himself we get no picture of the society which lies at the conclusion of history.

Since the late eighteenth century, in opposition to all governmentalist conceptions of ethical society, various writers have urged the possibility and desirability of an anarchist society. Anarchist movements, aiming at the abolition of government and the initiation of a reign of freedom and voluntary cooperation, have from time to time constituted a serious threat to institutions of government, violence, oppression and exploitation. In our day, after a period in which historians had come to speak of anarchism as a movement and idea of the past, available for post-mortem examination, it is beginning to be realized that the extreme centralization of governmental authority may have finally become self-defeating and that political collectivism, whether 'communist' or 'democratic', may be incompatible not only with the values of self-realization and personal freedom, not only with economic justice and ethical society, but perhaps also with continued human existence. As criticism of and rebellion against mass society has become more intense, anarchism has once more become 'historical'. It is difficult to understand how students of political theory can continue any longer to disregard the logically obvious alternative of anarchism.

What is this alternative, concretely? Anarchism has always been anti-ideological; anarchists have always insisted on the priority of life and action to theory and system. Subjection to a theory implies in practice subjection to an authority (a party) which interprets the theory authoritatively, and this subjection would fatally undermine the intention of creating a society without central political authority. Thus no anarchist writings are authoritative or definitive in the sense that Marx's writings have been regarded by his followers. Nevertheless, one is entitled to ask whether the anarchists can indicate credible means by which a society organized on principles of voluntary cooperation can deal with very well-known problems of social existence. Otherwise anarchism would be idle fantasy.

Giovanni Baldelli's book is a sketch of one anarchist's answer. 'A sketch', because the present volume, in the preparation of which it has been my pleasure to assist the author, is an abridgement, for purposes of publication, of a much longer book; many subsidiary topics have necessarily been omitted. 'Of one anarchist', because, since anarchism can have no official doctrine, it can have no official spokesman. On certain important matters Baldelli differs considerably from most other anarchists, above all with respect to economic questions. But anarchists have always differed on these issues, and Baldelli's theory which the reader will find here, may represent a decided advance upon the two theories most favoured by anarchists, the anarchist-communism of Kropotkin and the anarcho-syndicalism adopted by the Spanish anarchist movement. The reader who wishes to understand the ethical basis of anarchism and to judge its practicality will find, therefore, that the author has attempted to solve many of the obvious difficulties in traditional anarchist thought. The reader who wants a general introduction to anarchism should also find the book entirely apt, because Baldelli is well qualified to provide such an introduction. Although an extremely independent thinker, he has been a participant from within the anarchist movement and from within the ethical community which this 'anti-power' movement has aspired to be.

What Baldelli has done, as I read him, is to return to that anarchist tradition which takes *ethical* premises as its point of departure – that tradition which reasons from a certain conception of 'right' and 'wrong' in social existence. In this Baldelli is akin to Proudhon, whose inquiries into justice and, correlatively, property, have remained the most deepgoing among anarchist thinkers. The primacy given to the ethical shapes the spirit of Baldelli's thoughts as it shaped that of Proudhon. The premises of Bakunin's anarchism, by contrast, were essentially *libertarian* in the sense that the concept of freedom came first; Max Stirner's anarchistic egoism, although different in philosophical basis and terminology, was in this respect close to Bakunin. In Bakuninism there is a natural tendency to think in essentially evolutionary terms and to regard anarchism as a movement of the extreme 'Left', which is why the French Marxist Daniel Guérin can find in Bakunin the crowning moment of anarchist theory and a valuable libertarian counterbalance to the authoritarian tendencies in Marxism. The Bakuninist way was not Proudhon's nor is it Baldelli's. A third major possibility within anarchism is to give priority to *eudemonistic* premises, to make happiness central, and to regard freedom and ethics as derivative. This was the vein of William Godwin, the author of the first major anarchist treatise; most recently it is the vein of Paul Goodman. The tendency of such anarchism is towards rapprochement with what stands politically to the 'right' of anarchism, namely liberalism. This is not Baldelli's way either.

It may be that with Errico Malatesta (1853–1932), in whose thought these three kinds of justification appear in synthesis, anarchism achieved its greatest balance, just by reason of the value-pluralism of the Malatestan vision. Even if that is true, and even if an ethical conception of anarchism is necessarily one sided, a careful re-study of ethical foundations is bound to be valuable. In his key concept of 'ethical capital', Baldelli has a 'middle term' by which to exhibit the link between the idea of ethical society and the idea of anarchism. By means of this middle term he is able to open new perspectives on many problems: the nature of authority and freedom, which Baldelli regards as complementary rather than antithetical; of value and exploitation; of law; of the anti-power struggle. (Underlying these analyses is a theme, crucial to the whole analysis, which the careful reader will notice in a variety of contexts, the theme of *faith* in the 'ethical capital'.) If the link which Baldelli creates between ethics and anarchism is firm – and this I will not prejudge – he will have made a significant contribution to both our thought about the ethical life and our thought about anarchism.

David T. Wieck

Acknowledgements

This book was first conceived and written as an extensive treatise with chapters on such matters as religion, education and defence, all from the point of view of an anarchist society. The reduction and selection of the material leading to its present form is the work of David Wieck. His are the suggestions that have given the book its new organic form; to him are due also many improvements of syntax and phrasing. I am particularly grateful to him for the true anarchist spirit with which he has undertaken this work, for his scrupulous respect for the thought in the original material, and for that generosity of selfhood with which he took upon himself even such jobs as the retyping of the manuscript and the correction of proofs. To have the book prefaced by him is a great service to the reader, for no one is more familiar with its contents than he, and it is an honour for the author, as David Wieck is and was an anarchist at a time when anarchism was far from fashionable, even among the rebels.

Introduction

Anarchism is the purity of rebellion. A pig who struggles wildly and rends the air with his cries while he is held to be slaughtered, and a baby who kicks and screams when, wanting warmth and his mother's breast, he is made to wait in the cold – these are two samples of natural rebellion. Natural rebellion always inspires either deep sympathy and identification with the rebelling creature, or a stiffening of the heart and an activation of aggressive-defensive mechanisms to silence an accusing truth. This truth is that each living being is an end in itself; that nothing gives a being the right to make another a mere instrument of his purposes. The rebel against authority holds to this truth in everything that concerns him and recognizes no other judge than himself.

Natural rebellion is an outburst of energy against constriction, a statement of a will whose identity and integrity are threatened, and it aims at nothing more than removing an obstacle or breaking free from a cage. But natural rebellion can be a shortcut to tyranny. Not every rebel is an anarchist. The man experienced in rebellion knows how to forestall it in others; the professional rebel assimilates the mentality and methods of the oppressor, to which he may even have felt a strong attraction from the start.

Rebellion can act as an illumination and when that happens, and faith is kept, the rebel becomes an anarchist. For the anarchist, rebellion is not only a statement of *will* but a statement of *rightness* and *truth*. It is such a statement if the truth and rightness of rebellion are recognized for others as well as for oneself; if no words are spoken against other men's truth; and if nothing is done to others that, done to oneself, would cause one to rebel.

Because oppression takes many forms, anarchists have often stressed one or another particular motive for rebellion so passionately as to obscure their original inspiration. Anarchism is not a philosophy. A man's philosophy is his way of giving unity and coherence to his thoughts, and if he is asked to organize his thoughts other than as he himself chooses, the demand is in contradiction to anarchism. But if it is not a philosophy, anarchism is far more than rebellion. As is suggested by its being an 'ism', it rests on more than one intuition and embraces a variety of methods and actions. The truth that is so vivid in the experience of rebellion does not cease to be true once rebellion is spent. If rebellion sought to defend something worthwhile, there must be values of which it is the defender.

Anarchism must rest on fundamental principles that are the result of an act of choice and are operative as an act of faith, regardless of whether they may be fitted into one philosophical system or another or whether they may have received rational and even scientific support. The context of these principles is the interplay of human actions, and their function is to give unity of style to a person's life and judgements. Since no single authority can decide what is or is not anarchist, and since anarchists can be recognized only by their allegiance to anarchist principles, the latter require clear and unequivocal statement.

The human person is primary

The individual alone is a seat of consciousness. Without individuals there are no historical or social events, no forces or entities, with which mankind could be concerned. God, race, country, State, class, history, progress, party are creations of individual minds and have no reality outside them; to none of them may the individual be sacrificed. That such entities are invoked when the sacrifice of an individual is sought, means that they are functioning as a justification of murder, as a mask for expediency and self-interest. The mortality of individuals, and the immortality or relative immortality of God or State or history, may be felt to justify the sacrifice of the individual. But if a man is told that he is nothing but an ephemeral piece of dirt, he can reply: Precisely because I must die, and know it, I can engulf all such entities now into that nothingness which will be mine only when I die.

Human life is sacred

Man creates his own values, his own rational and affective attachments, and his own motives for action. To live is not enough, he needs reasons to live. But without life there are no reasons to live, no values. Life, therefore, as the essential condition of all values, must be cherished above them all, and must be held sacred. Any counter-argument is invalid because the mind that advances the argument would not be there if life were not respected. Sacredness is a religious concept but nothing less is sufficient to resist ideas, attitudes and actions that make life cheap and replaceable and of only a functional or numerical value. As sacred, human life must not be destroyed, or played with, or impaired, or wilfully and callously exposed to affliction.

Coercion must be rejected

Every organism possesses the motive force and equipment necessary to cope with its milieu. For man this milieu includes society, and when society protects each and all of its members it exercises its function. Coercion, whether by society or individuals, runs counter to the needs and purposes of the individual and is therefore evil. It forces a human being to behave according to the needs, feelings, thoughts and will of another, as if he had none himself; he must use some of his most precious energies to distort and modify his own being. Of course, the individual must not be a parasite upon society, but instinctual promptings, reason and love are capable of assuring social order; coercion, on the other hand, is needed by and is the resort of the anti-social, the parasite and the mistrustful.

The end does not justify the means

The tree is known by its fruit but the so-called ends of political organizations and movements seem never to manage to ripen. Let the tree be judged, then, by what it feeds upon, the so-called means. To say that the end justifies the means is to acknowledge that the means, judged separately, are unjust. If they are unjust, it is because there are concepts of justice prior to, and independent of, the ends to be realized. What will not be permissible tomorrow is permitted today in order that it not be permitted tomorrow. This is to declare today's humanity in some way inferior to tomorrow's, and to burden the latter with a debt of gratitude unasked for and more likely to be cursed than blessed.

Double standards are unacceptable

Moral standards have played an important part in shaping the life of societies to the benefit of most of their members. With the sharpening of class consciousness and the increasing militancy and militarization of political ideologies, the same practices have come to be judged good or bad according to how they affect one's own or some opposite ideological camp. Different vocabularies are used to make the same practices appear essentially different in the two cases. Belonging to one society or section of society rather than another is mainly an accident of birth, and a truly moral standard abstracts from such accidents. In particular, no one is to be disqualified as a human being by the label of 'enemy'. What the enemy does to us and what we do to him must be weighed by the same scales and described by the same vocabulary.

Basic principles must be as few as possible so as to avoid theoretical and practical contradictions. Thus we have not listed among the basic principles above that 'human nature is fundamentally good' or that 'right and wrong are not decided by history'. One may behave as an anarchist and not believe that man is good; and although any subordination of right and wrong to history is a subordination to might, unacceptable to an anarchist, he could conceivably regard anarchist principles as valid only for his time and the future. 'The State must be abolished' is a corollary to the principle condemning coercion. 'Workers' control' and other anarchist slogans are similarly contingent.

Workers' control may be chosen by some anarchists as part of an anarchist-inspired economic structure but may be rejected by others: the workers themselves may not want it, and a different economic structure might be more efficient and ethically equal or superior. Anarchism, in fact, cannot be linked to a particular economic system. Justice is social rather than economic, and injustice and oppression are compatible with any economic system so far devised. There can be no freedom where the modes of production and consumption are decided on any grounds other than a particular society's needs and resources. That economic questions are important, and that talk of freedom to a starving man is idle, no anarchist will deny, but for anarchists it is not a question of giving today's poor either freedom *or* enough to eat, but of finding a way for them to have both freedom *and* enough to eat. Enough to eat for everybody must, and can, be provided without coercion. The economic system acceptable to anarchists is one free from coercion; its name and particular modes of operation are of secondary importance. Economy subordinated to ethics and not controlled by power – that is the anarchist formula.

If such are the aims of anarchists, why does the man in the street see anarchism as an endorsement of all that is socially disruptive? Why does he not see in men inspired by anarchist principles his best friends and ultimately his greatest hope? Why is it not realized that in order to be truly social one has to be an anarchist?

Chiefly responsible for the bad name of anarchism are the supporters of political power, but anarchists too have contributed by being vague and perfunctory concerning the social side of their doctrine and by frequently espousing the cause of rebellion without insisting on its social illumination. Anti-social impulses and practices may only too easily find in anarchism a pseudo-rational justification. For these reasons the adjective 'social' is a useful addition to the word 'anarchism' – in order to be truly anarchist one has to be social.

Rebellion presupposes the existence of oppression and, on the psychological plane, deification of rebellion creates an affective compact with oppression. Experience teaches that ugliness and horror are most rife in a struggle against them. He who needs something to rebel against is less of a social anarchist than he who seeks to create something against which there is no need to rebel. There may be no end to the ugly, sordid and horrifying things against which an honest man cannot help but revolt, but there are also things that are beautiful, joyful and pure. If it were wrong to attend to the latter while the former still thrive, then a hopeless perpetual struggle would become the only meaning of life.

A myth has arisen that the oppressors are few and the oppressed many and that all that is needed to end oppression is for the many to get rid of the few. The myth has led to contempt for the passive oppressed who do not rebel overtly – contempt, that is, for the common man, the bulk of mankind. It is fashionable to present hate and contempt for humanity as the exasperation and despair of compassion, but in that case rebellion should be against existence itself. When a man who is horrified by the basic evil of the world and his own existence, and who sees no God to rebel against, takes revenge on his fellow beings, he is a coward and a hypocrite. Perhaps the ugly, sordid and horrifying things of which there is no end have always been produced by hypocritical and cowardly rebellion against existence, but that is not the rebellion of the social anarchist.

'Social anarchism' means that anarchism is intended to be for the good of society, not for the exploitation of society. More explicitly it means that men are not to be moulded or bludgeoned into an abstract scheme called anarchism, but that because they want certain things and hold certain things dear they will find in anarchism the best system to safeguard them.

Every man, in so far as he belongs to his society, is conservative, and the word 'society' applies particularly to those activities which can most aptly be compared to the circulatory, respiratory and digestive functions of a living body. Anything that disturbs such activities is contrary to health. In the consciousness of each of its members and in the reality of their life-serving interchanges, a society keeps its identity and continuity – as an individual keeps his – thanks to constancies and regularities and a modicum of security and satisfaction, not less vital for being referred to contemptuously by revolutionaries as 'bourgeois'. There is an order in society, of which parties of the Right claim to be the defenders, knowing that they can find a response in men of all classes, particularly among producers of prime necessities. Revolutionaries, like politicians, are apt to dismiss as irrelevant the fact that, while they are changing society and making history, production and essential services will be kept going by those who will suffer more immediately and more drastically from disruption than will revolutionaries or politicians.

It is not entirely surprising, therefore, that Proudhon, the anarchist with the keenest sense of social realities, should have been thought of as a man of the 'Right'. Other anarchists, while priding themselves on being mentally emancipated iconoclasts, have often bowed abjectly to the mystique of the 'Left'. Both Right and Left are systems of mystification and political exploitation; to a country, they are what superpowers are to the world, namely the premise and instrument of war – called 'civil' in the former case. Inevitably and significantly, any Left that is triumphant becomes the new Right, thus showing how false, and merely convenient, was its claim to represent the oppressed against the oppressors. Any man who genuinely cares for his society will keep clear of any alignment of Right against Left or vice versa, just as a pacifist will have nothing to do with armies arrayed to slaughter one another.

Too many reactionary governments have been established in the name of revolution for the social anarchist to identify reaction with the Right and revolution with the Left. Nor will the anarchist seek revolution for its own sake. If he did, he would be *against* a host of things but *for none*. except for finding his own self-realization in conflict. A truly anarchist and social revolution will not be the work of revolutionaries but of society itself.

The professional revolutionary cannot be anarchist because he has two vocabularies and two sets of standards. While he speaks of freedom and happiness, he relegates them to the future. What he wants and offers now is a struggle for power, discipline, and all the excitements and hazards of civil war. It is time to apply to the mystique of revolution the same critical intelligence that has been applied to the mystique of war. The liberation of society and the individual cannot be effected without bringing to an end any mystique that demands their sacrifice. A dedication to the absolute of Revolution, chosen for oneself and willed for others, is no less an alienation of self than that imposed by other absolutes such as God, the Fatherland, the Race, the Dialectics of History or the Working Class.

Very few people find the meaning of life in surrender to an absolute. People do not want to fight in order to live, or live in order to fight; they simply want to draw from life some sensual or other pleasure, and to achieve some measure of fulfilment in love, companionship, service and creative work. For the sake of these they surrender each day some of their time and energies to the demands of a life-negating system, of whose life-negation they are often more aware than the revolutionaries themselves because they often suffer from it more directly. They also usually have enough sense not to believe in miracles, and to perceive that, after the revolution, life-negating demands will still be made upon them, while in the process they may lose whatever they hold dear, and life itself.

In contrast to the revolution proclaimed by the professional revolutionaries, an anarchist revolution is one of generalized rebellion, without leaders and masses. Each social unit shakes off the fetters and mechanisms imposed on it by political and economic powers. An anarchist revolution may be violent, but not of necessity. The revolution is of society, by society and for society, and the degree of violence will depend on the volume, obstinacy and resources of the antisocial forces that oppose the revolution. State and capitalist machines can crack at any and all of their joints. Many men now holding key or subordinate positions in structures of oppression and exploitation could come to see themselves as social beings first and foremost, and act accordingly.

If sufficient wisdom and social consciousness have been attained so that violence from any quarter is regarded with abhorrence, revolution could take the form of the anarchization of a democracy, by the gradual abolition of laws and of rules and regulations based on political power. Each law could be suspended for a trial period, and if the evil and inconveniences it was supposed to prevent did not occur, or if there were positive gains from the suspension, that would be proof that, as far as the particular law was concerned, the people were ready for anarchy.

The paths to anarchy, it can be seen, are many, as they should be, but none of them is a shortcut. Anarchy will come if, and when, and only in so far as, it is wanted. To want it is the first step and, in a sense, that step is a realization of anarchy. For the will to anarchy not to be wasted, divided, turned against itself or betrayed, ideas concerning an anarchist society and the essential conditions of freedom should be as clear as possible. Clear ideas are the surest bastion against fraudulence and malicious nonsense. This is a book of ideas. If the reader does not always find them clear, we trust that he will be helped to form clearer ones of his own, and thus be better equipped than he was before to detect fraudulence and malicious nonsense, however learnedly disguised, and however militantly and engagingly presented.

Part One **The Ethical Capital**

Chapter One **Good Will**

Whatever in human relationships is neither violent nor in any way injurious, and whatever dictates to one man actions which are beneficial to another, is a contribution to what we shall call the ethical capital of mankind.

Skilfully invested, ethical capital brings regular and increasing dividends, which may be spent immediately or reinvested. It may also, unfortunately, be ravaged or utterly destroyed. Some have seen signs that it is subject to cyclical variation. Because it cannot be measured; because it can be transmitted without diminution; because it is both potential and actual, never acquired once and for all, and never definable without reference to ideal standards; and because it is affixed more to the meanings of actions than to the actions themselves – for these reasons it would not be improper to call it spiritual. We prefer to call it ethical because it is an agglomerate of wills directed to good purposes and socially beneficial.

In asserting that goodness, i.e. ethical capital, is real, we do not assert that man is wholly good, nor do we deny the reality of war, slavery and exploitation. It will be enough that in human society there is, as well as evil, clearly discernible goodness. The social life of man gives abundant evidence of this. Observance of custom and law cannot be imagined as resting entirely on fear of punishment. Although many laws perpetuate advantages gained by antecedent violence and apply unequally to rich and poor, and although most are outwardly prohibitive and therefore negative, they rest on the positive basis of the will of most men to live peacefully together. Customs, if not laws, are a necessary and fundamental feature of social existence, made by human will before they in turn set restraints upon that will. Social existence entails a host of renunciations and sacrifices that, however painful, men accept for the comfort of being members of society, or because they are convinced of their necessity and desirability, or because they see the justice of a general distribution of duties and sacrifices. Such recognition of the needs of social existence is universally regarded as a mark of adulthood.

Written history usually concentrates upon the infinite ways and means by which men do violence to one another. Unquestionably, violence has played a part in keeping some societies together and in allowing them to survive in competition with others. The part played by the renunciation of violence is much greater, however, if less spectacular and less visible to historians. About the relative importance of love and of coercion in the origins of society, speculation would be useless. We have sufficient grounds, however, for affirming that love, its rational substitute in the form of morals, and its transcendent sanction in the form of religion, are the factors chiefly responsible for peaceful living and for every freedom that is not a disguised tyranny. Without general willingness to live peacefully, and without all the sacrifices and renunciations this willingness prompts and sustains, civilizations and their immense fruits would hardly be conceivable.

To understand the nature of ethical capital more fully, the coefficients of human goodness must be examined in some detail. Let the behaviour of the good Samaritan be our starting point. His picking up of a wounded man, his healing, clothing and feeding him and providing him with shelter were the manifestations of a disposition that was present in the Samaritan and absent from the priest and the Levite who left the wounded man where he lay. Such a disposition to do good, exercised repeatedly, is called a virtue. In so far as others can rely on it, it is a social rather than an individual possession – invested, as it were, and put to productive use.

More social still, although no more virtuous than disposition to do good, is an extremely primitive form of ethical capital: the absence, or effective restraint, of disposition to do evil. It is obvious that no freedom is possible without restraint on the part of all others; even less possible is property, which Locke named as freedom's correlative. Indeed, human society would be impossible without restraint, particularly of the kind that is self-imposed.

To be sure, if desires are tempered and curtailed solely from self-interest or fear, self-restraint is mere biological expediency or part of the mechanisms of power, and not ethical. Such unethical origins can be recognized when changes in the mechanics of power, or new opportunities, lead to the disappearance of restraints which did not stem from ethical intention and were not harmonized with an ethical whole. Nevertheless, restraint which was originally a virtue out of biological necessity must be counted as ethical when it continues to operate after the circumstances and motives that begot it are gone.

Conscience, and therefore all moral life, has been disparaged as necessity turned into virtue – we are virtuous, it is said, because originally it did not pay, or took too much daring, to be bad. Such a view assumes that every social influence on the development of ethical habits possesses some form of retributive power, when in fact biologically founded patterns of example and imitation would seem to determine at least as many types of behaviour as does the pattern of punishment and reward.

Psychoanalysis has popularized the notion that anti-social dispositions are due to experiences of harm suffered or witnessed in childhood. It has not stressed equally the complementary notion that kind dispositions may result from acts of goodness of which one was beneficiary or witness. It would be extraordinary if subconscious memory worked exclusively or preferentially on instances of evil. All in all, acts of kindness and tokens of friendliness received during childhood far outweigh acts of unkindness and hostility, and can be regarded as one source of our ethical capital. Gratitude resulting from having been the object of loving attention is thus a kind of primitive accumulation of ethical capital. Though proverbially difficult to find, especially when demanded, gratitude is not really scarce; like hatred and resentment, it is deflected, projected and diffused, so that it seldom goes back to those to whom it is due.

Allied to gratitude is reverence for the old and admiration for the best representative of the group. Cool tolerance, disrespect and contempt for the old have been in the ascendant only in the last seven or eight generations, mainly under the impact of the industrial revolution. As repositories and transmitters of knowledge who were able to show a long record of achievement, the old used to excite veneration and wonder, contagious emotions that leave, on subsiding, a disposition of respect.

A child may be told what to respect and admire, but what finally decides him to respect and admire certain things and persons is that he sees his teachers and other members of his community moved by these feelings; a halo gathers around such persons and things and sets them apart. Once acquired, reverence and respect may be extended to other objects and acts as catalysts of idealization. The kind and degree of civilization of any society are best shown by the type of persons and things it thus reveres and admires. In such patterns we can see both the continuity and the means of growth of ethical capital.

A god or cluster of gods is the supreme object of respect and veneration that expresses a society's faith in itself. When traditional religions weakened, the need was felt to retain the function fulfilled by the godhead, and a leader or prophet or hypostatized abstraction was treated as divine. Of all forms of religion, totemism expressed most directly the feeling of a divine element within society itself. In all religions, however, the devotion of the individual to society and its gods is abundantly testified. When societies were vastly dissimilar and had little contact except in raids and war, to be ejected from the society of one's birth was nearly as dreadful as death itself, and even today exile is a painful experience.

Of the many factors that attach an individual to the land and people of his birth, all or nearly all of which stem from the ethical capital of the society, none is so operative as the ethical capital itself, none as vital as faith in its existence and permanence. Faith in other people develops earlier and is more necessary to survival than faith in oneself. As it is more precarious, it needs constant reassurance. Whatever their specific purposes, things done together – hunting, warring, eating, learning, praying, dancing – are reassuring, as their repetition and ritualization show. Notions of right and wrong, and their supporting beliefs, vary from society to society, but confidence in these ideas depends on their being shared with the other members of one's society. Social cohesion is therefore not simply a biological fact or a function of economic interest but rests on the sharing of common values, and there is a correlation between the veneration and respect a society has for its values and the attachment to society felt by each of its members.

An ant, taken away from its hill, is so upset and bewildered that it forgets to feed, and dies. Though inclined to despise such an extreme, man is himself gregarious to a degree, and to understand his ethical needs one must understand the nature of his relation to his fellows.

The full meaning of human gregariousness is not apparent under modern conditions. Imagine how early man must have felt when, severed by some accident from the little world of his birth, he saw himself the only human in a world of rocks and trees, rushing waters, blazing sun or threatening ice, strange animals by day and stranger shadows by night. We complain that it is impossible for any two human beings fully to understand and communicate with each other, but far greater is man's incapability of understanding other creatures. Fear of the unknown and aversion to dumb and unpredictable surroundings have been as decisive as any other factors in bringing men together. In myth and ritual, religions have enshrined the sense of guilt that early man experienced in daring to create modes of existence unlike those of other creatures, and in achieving at their expense a measure of happiness and power that he was not sure was permitted by the lords of creation.

The great difference between living with other men and being surrounded by things inhuman is that only a conscious being such as man can acknowledge consciousness in another and recognize him as an autonomous being with thoughts and feelings of his own; only by understanding others does he understand himself. This recognition of others' subjectivity is an essential feature of all phases of social existence that are not purely biological or a product of the mechanisms of power.

Other people's subjectivity is at first apprehended intuitively and imaginatively. Later it attests its presence in reason, memory, volition and inhibition. Whereas anything that treats us as an object seems to shrink and darken our self, a mind aware and respectful of ours has an expanding and brightening effect. Strictly speaking, the coincidence of two minds, two centres of will and sensibility, never occurs. Yet poetry, philosophy and religion are most eloquent when stating its possibility, and they could not have attained their high degree of development unless there were experiences in which this coincidence is approximated.

Such experiences, though different in kind and intensity, have a common feature, usually defined as love. One centre of subjectivity is a beam of light falling on another; it apprehends, anticipates and helps shape the other's intentions, and supports their realization. Love, as the attempt on the part of one person to shift his centre of awareness, is the prime and ultimate source of ethical life.

The prototype of love thus defined is that of a mother for her child. It is instinctive, biologically rooted, and to some extent compulsive. Though slighted by the religious-minded and the reason-proud, this first love is unrivalled in developing man's fondness for his kind, and in showing him how to care for others without concern for immediate and precise advantage. The love of a mother for her child may so wrench and transpose her existence that she can be said to live for and by her child; she can die to save her child, and, should she lose it, she may even hasten or welcome her death. A mother's love can put meaning and faith into even the most wretched of lives. A man who can remember, however dimly, how much he meant for his mother, will never quite believe that it does not matter whether he lives or not, or whether he lives one way or another.

The love of a man and a woman is also not limited to the exercise of a biological function. Except in conditions of continual excitation and too easy satisfaction, the sexual impulse manifests its power by hurling the self out of its normal orbit. While most other impulses are centripetal, life-preserving, the sexual impulse is centrifugal to the point where it may send the organism headlong to death. Even when it is not yet love, it is ethically relevant if its object is not discarded as soon as it has given satisfaction. A man who keeps a woman with a view to future satisfaction, for example, is regarding her as a thing, but if he is as much as aware of her independent will and takes it into account, although he may only wish to ensure that she will still serve him, a certain contribution is made to the ethical capital, if none to love. As soon as he goes out of his way to meet her wishes he is treating her as a person and is moving in the direction of the ethical.

Human behaviour takes a more markedly ethical direction when, as an offshoot, extension, deviation or copy of the maternal and mating instincts, it becomes concerned with the protection of the weak and the undefended. When evil propensities are held in check in oneself and chastised in others, the purely biological is firmly superseded and the mechanics of power are undermined. Those authors who applied the theory of the survival of the fittest to human beings overlooked the role played by protection of the weak. It is strange too that fraternity should have been chosen generally as the ethical feeling *par excellence* when benevolent feelings towards strangers are often more like feelings for one's children, one's parents and grandparents, than like those for one's brothers.

Supporters of the ethical capital are not exclusively the weak and the aged, the female and the slave, as has been claimed by ideologies flattering the strong. The aged and the weak, the sick and the maimed, have the greatest immediate interest in the preservation of the ethical capital, but the young and the strong contribute to it. Promotion of the ethical cause does not come only from poverty and defeat, nor is the cause promoted only by restraint and renunciation. Nobility too creates and embodies ethical values, for there is a will to give which is more 'super-human' and god-like than the will to power, freer from fear, less hampered by accident and necessity, less shackled by the weight of past achievements.

Generosity and liberality are the two virtues through which a will to give is constant. Their names show them to be the privilege of the best and the free. The will to power is miserly, spiteful and rude, while the will to give is joyous and refined. They may both exist in the same man; in political contests they intertwine and try to bring each other to heel, and it is not true that power always has the last word. While generosity of self is abroad, power is never secure. The man generous to the point of laying down his life for an ideal is an abiding threat to the life of a tyrant. A hopeful fact amid many grim others is that the most repressive measures of modern systems of tyranny are not aimed so much at subjection of rival powers as at forestalling the blows that are feared from the nobly inspired.

The will to live does not coincide with the will to power, and power is but one province of the whole kingdom of life. Granted that intelligence developed originally as an instrument, it does not follow that it should or can be no more than a handmaiden of power. It appears, rather, as life's crowning and surpassing purpose – or, if one pleases, as a splendid luxury.

If we must explain everything in terms of will, then intelligence is a will to know. Just as we can seek knowledge in order to be powerful, we can exercise power in order to know. External stimuli may prompt its exercise but its inner force is a will to think. Again, although the fruits of the thought may be put to any kind of use, their mere attainment may be sufficient and satisfying. People are not rare who ask no more from their intelligence than the shaping of thoughts, or the joining of them in patterns, or the finding of means to make them intelligible to others. The laws of thought and language are not those of life and power. Delight in intelligence has been explained away as compensation for the unfit in the struggle for power, as escape for the fearful, as solace to the conquered. But the fundamental discovery of intelligence is that defeat comes anyway in the end, that success in a struggle for power lies not in doing what one wants but in wanting what can most surely be done, and that there is not much point in being intelligent if intelligence is to remain enslaved to the crudest biological needs and the mechanics of power.

All exercises of intelligence that betoken freedom, all its achievements that are or can be rescued from selfish and destructive purposes, all the sciences and arts, are so many stones and houses for the ethical city. To be human is to know of a world where the laws of power and biological need do not rule invariantly – a world of harmony instead of strife, of intelligent creativeness rather than of stupidity and destruction.

Specially favourable conditions of climate, prosperity and peace make men pause from their ordinary pursuits, release them from their tensions, and reveal to them that it is both possible and worthwhile to cultivate modes of behaviour that do not fall under the category of the necessary or useful but under that of the beautiful and pleasant. The same revelation may also be gained under severe conditions of struggle against nature or other men. Jealousy, fear and rivalry between the sexes have in some societies led men to impose upon their women a system of upbringing that enhances gentle characteristics, and women have sometimes reacted by showing preference for men who share similar characteristics or who approach them with least inward contempt. The dangers of rivalry between young and old, combined with awareness of mutual dependence and sympathetic links, have engendered customs which, besides preventing or

checking murderous impulses, have developed a taste for behaviour free from hatred and violence. Finally, frequent
contact with people outside one's household and neighbourhood, the result of the building of towns and development of
trade, long ago made it imperative to drop hostile forms of
behaviour, both to secure the advantages for which trade developed and cities were built, and to economize on aggressive
energies.

Thus the virtues of gentleness and politeness were born.
Their social importance may readily be grasped by realizing
that even when they are known to be but a thin veneer one is
thankful for them and unwilling to face the ugliness of what
they cover up or of what would soon replace them. Appreciation of these virtues, in oneself or others, for their own
sake and the advantages they bring, contributes positively to
social living. A sign of their social value is the high
refinement they have reached in societies far from conspicuous in other respects for their ethical behaviour. The
fact that exquisite sensitiveness, charm, kindness and beautiful manners are found side by side with cruelty, brutality
and cold-bloodedness is not a proof of the fundamental rot-
tenness of human nature, but an intimation of the necessity
to break down barriers between races, nations and classes.
Granting that the main incentive to refinement is an urge to
excel and achieve distinction, the suppression of reputedly
inferior beings and the adoption of savage and barbarous
ways in dealing with them is an indication that courage to
achieve distinction is in fact lacking. Nothing is more
common, and nothing less distinctive, than for the strong to
abuse the weak, or to kill them.

Though not itself part of the ethical capital, weakness is,
as it were, ethical raw material. Ethicality is hardly conceivable among animals that are perfectly healthy. The rule
among them is to get rid of weaklings and the maimed. On
the other hand, it is a lesson of experience that it does not
pay a weak person to look for fights with people stronger
than he. When he has no choice but to live with the strong,
it is in the interest of the weak to develop conventions,

customs and institutions that control or exclude the us
force. Force is not itself creative, and when it is made the
ultimate determinant of all questions, it needs to be tested
constantly; groups that rely on it for survival tend soon to be
destroyed physically or to be corrupted and to decay. Thus a
so-called slave morality may eventually permeate a society;
and force, although retained, is kept in the background and
its representatives made to occupy a subordinate position.

Hand in glove with slave morality go religions of death –
religions based on the mortality and frustration of man, on
his final defeat and his inevitable surrender of everything he
has acquired. Illnesses and misfortunes – one's own or
others – are a premonition of death and cast a disintegrating
light on the natural and conventional purposes of life that
had been taken for granted. It takes intelligence to realize
the omnipotence of death, courage to accept it as a permanent guest in one's thoughts, and character to build a
style of life according to the new meanings that things have
when seen in the aspect of eternity. So it is not necessarily
the cowardly and the weak of body, will and mind who live
by a slave morality or a religion of death. By the imprint
such moralities and religions have left on contemporary and
succeeding generations, an imprint far exceeding anything
achieved by force, the contrary conclusion would seem the
more correct.

As fascination with evil is associated with exuberance of
vital spirits and ability to strike, so evil's opposite presents
itself as the natural alternative when vital spirits are at low
ebb and power is lacking. Goodness as a virtue, as a rational
aim and inner discipline, comes from reflection on one's own
limitations, brought home by the demise of a relative, an
illness, a reverse of fortune, or a defeat in serious or playful
competition. Without experience of suffering and harm received, natural intuitive imagination hardly stands a chance
to rule the mind and admonish the will ethically. That is
why one can hurt and even kill without a pang. There
would be no goodness if we had no organs of suffering, and
knew of no weakness in ourselves.

Confronted by the weak and the undefended, it depends only on ourselves whether we shall injure them or not, delight in doing them harm, or spare them and do them good. It is in respect to them that problems of ethics arise. In respect to the strong, on the other hand, any attempted harmful action is an act of courage, and courage is a virtue that excites admiration. For this reason, public actions against the weak are presented as highly courageous, by attributing powers to the weak that they obviously have not. The burning of lonely old women as witches, the liquidation of Jews as conspiring against the rest of the world, the disposal of unorthodox communists as fascist and capitalist agents, are examples of this cowardly and hypocritical conduct.

At the transmitting end, evil is not experienced as evil. When he experiences it at the receiving end, the reflective person feels repugnance to joining those forces in nature and society that cause suffering and sorrow. Death, recognized as the power that infinitely transcends every human power, as the darkness to which every light of intelligence and glow of things desired must finally submit, assumes such a fearful quality that to inflict it on anybody appears at once the height of stupidity and the most criminal usurpation. For some, the thought of death, while robbing life of enchantment and preventing acts of will from acquiring momentum, reveals that a peace is to be found in the practice of detachment, in communion and understanding, and in experience of an inner union among all things outwardly at strife; this peace amply repays the loss of pleasures and ambitions voluntarily surrendered. Such peace gives the throbbing certainty that the casting off of self in acts of goodness is man's supreme achievement and has consequences reaching far into the ultimate purpose of things. Whether attaining the perfection of the mystic's abnegation, or existing as the short-lived mood of a sick or wounded man who forgives his enemies and forsakes his possessions, death-inspired self-detachment has produced fruits of goodness as beneficial to the human race as any coming from other sources.

When the thought of death does not create a psychology of detachment, it may still produce ethical results by the pathos it infuses into human attachments. A person loved in full awareness of his mortality is more deeply and intensely dear than when loved in the heedlessness of natural attraction. Upon the death of a person with whom one has lived, pity touches the heart and one regrets not having been kinder and more helpful to him while he was alive. Familiarity with the thought of death, and mindfulness of other people's mortality, can make us feel pity for them while they are still alive, even when they appear most intractable and stupid. Pity has often been described as a selfish feeling, as a luxury of the fortunate and a pleasant guilt-quencher. But we believe it to be rooted in an intuition of the sameness of all living creatures in the face of death. Clumsy and powerless as it may often be against physical causes of human suffering, it is man's most redeeming feature.

Chapter Two **Exploitation**

Ethics and economics are intimately connected but not as a one-sided connection of cause and effect. On the one hand, the Samaritan could not have done his good deed merely out of a good disposition – without money, clothes or mount. If he were to come across a wounded man each time he made a journey, he would soon run out of money and clothes; the more wounded men he attended to, the less opportunity would he have to earn the resources to help them; in time he would take another route or behave like the Priest and the Levite. On the other hand, the Priest and the Levite, though perhaps ten times richer than the Samaritan and fully able to help, were not ethically disposed to help the wounded man.

Every productive activity presupposes an ethical disposition – negatively, because it is an alternative to plundering, positively, because it provides someone else with means of subsistence, tools, amenities, services. Except in the manufacture of poisons and weapons, production is life-serving and causes no harm. When the normal and original aims of production are subordinated to the profit motive, productive activity becomes plagued with anti-ethical, exploitative features. It is also plagued when by legal and other means a monopoly of raw materials, markets or producers' goods is secured. However, in these cases it is the conditions of production that are distorted and anti-ethical, not the productive activity itself.

Something of an ethical quality adheres to products as well. Of this the poets are the natural interpreters in their discovery and statement of the spirituality of man-made things, from a loaf of bread to an engine. As production becomes progressively dehumanized and standardized, the songs about man-made things become elegiac or down-right deprecatory. Similarly, the man in the street becomes insensitive to the spirituality of things around him as his sense of wonder is blunted by increasingly complex and artificial conditions. The intricacies of the modern economic process, and its subordination to purposes of enrichment, to political rivalries, vanities and war, help make man-made things spiritually hollow. Produced with no respect for man, in turn they cease to be respected by man.

This destruction of spiritual meanings reduces the ethical capital; by no means does increase in the material wealth of a country safeguard the ethical wealth from depletion. Economic exploitation also is an exploitation of the ethical will, of the ethical disposition that productive activity presupposes. In economic exploitation not only are the worker's energies, time and skills alienated but his pacific and generous disposition, his trust, are exploited. The consequences are far-reaching; the ethical sentiments tend to dry up at their sources, and their opposites replace them.

For a man tends to treat others as he is himself treated. One is never wholly or unalterably good or bad. What is potentially good or bad, society helps bring (or prevents from being brought) to realization. In order to understand the connection between ethics and politics, between the moral life of an individual and that of the social system in which he lives, it will help to think of each man as possessed of a fund of ethical power that must be constantly renewed, just as his body needs to absorb at least as many calories as it spends. Faith is what a man feeds on ethically. Although biologically rooted, and thought by some to be divine in origin, this faith depends on society. Faith in God is an attempt to make the stock of a man's ethical power unlimited and independent of circumstances, and this faith may indeed help a man sustain his ethical capital through severe and protracted exploitation. But if we concluded that exploitation is therefore not destructive of the good life, we would forget that ethics draws its meaning from a social context. Faith of a more or less mystic kind is rare, and the ethical disposition of a man must ordinarily be sustained by its being reciprocated, and by his moving in a world where ethics obtains.

We know very well that if the wounded man knocks the good Samaritan over the head as soon as he recovers, and steals his money and mount, the Samaritan will not be kind again too readily to a wounded man. Jesus's injunction to turn the left cheek to him who has smitten you on the right, and to give your shirt to him who robs you of your coat, is not only contrary to natural impulses but is likely actually to diminish the ethical capital. If one submits to a second dose of violence after he has survived the first, he will be more in need of a kind neighbour's services than in a position to give help, and if one gives his shirt to the bully who has deprived him of his coat, he will have nothing to give to children who are shivering with cold. From a social viewpoint this teaching of Jesus' acquires value only if the action succeeds in changing the heart of the violent. Except in pious legends, such a change, if it occurs, is seldom durable, and there is no record that slavery as an institution has anywhere been ended by the slaves' forbearance and forgiveness.

The basic ethical fund of an individual is established by the kindness and training in kindness he receives in his formative years. More important still is the rate of assimilation and recuperation, similar to biological metabolism, by which his ethical structure is maintained. There occurs in everyday life a continual giving and taking of goodness, but there would soon be very little to give and take if the exchange were, so to speak, on a basis of cash payment and immediate consumption – if there were no credit open and no condoning of debts. Rules of politeness, when not themselves expressive of goodness, act as a kind of receipt of payment, an acknowledgement that goodness is the only recognizable tender.

The type of education that best serves the ethical cause is therefore one that enables a person to draw ethical energy from available and relatively invulnerable sources. The usual religious education stores the mind with precepts and examples made meaningful by a general vision of the purpose of the world and the destiny of man. As long as deceit or hypocrisy on the part of the educators is not suspected, the results of religious education are among the least exposed to damage from without. Religious education, however, inculcates responsibility of the soul to God, of the faithful to his Church, and never primarily of the individual to society and of society to the individual. Hardly interested in ending ethical exploitation, religious education fosters a mentality that finds servitude perfectly normal and does not scruple to force it upon others. Bound to a definite and rigid order of values, faith of a religious kind can be most intolerant of values that break or contradict that order, and as ruthless in dealing out persecution as heroic in withstanding it.

Persecution is never ethical. It is an instrument of power and not of right, an advantage taken over somebody. Ethical behaviour is for the protection of the weak – which means every man, for every man is weak, be it against illness and age or the ill will of other men. The weak may abuse good will, as a child does its mother's, but at their risk and peril, for they may lose the affection and regard bestowed on them and may call forth hostility on a plane where they are bound to lose. Except when the strong are divided and can be played off against each other, the tyranny of the weak is limited and can be easily shaken off. Deterioration of the ethical capital occurs chiefly at the hands of the strong, and, specifically, in their use of coercion to make men physically or psychologically incapable of acquiring and exercising an ethical disposition.

The worst kind of coercion, therefore, is the training or habituation of people to unethical actions. A practice of an institution is destructive of ethical capital when its cumulative effect does not simply scrape and dissolve the surface of a man's ethical disposition, robbing him, as it were, of his ethical pocket-money, but digs into his ethical savings by sapping the foundation of his faith in goodness. Exploitation of the ethical capital occurs when coercion is applied to elicit fruits of good will without giving anything in return. In fact this is the general meaning of exploitation: getting something for nothing or imposing a system from which one regularly gets more than he puts into it.

The practice of goodness is soon discouraged if he who

practises it is not recognized as good, or if his goodness fails to elicit it in others. Although decried as most improper for a good man to seek, there are in fact conditions in which deliberate goodness most naturally and healthily thrives. The effect on ethical disposition of lack of means, lack of acknowledgement, and lack of results, must be taken into account if we are to form an idea of the potential goodness of people. Encouraging goodness in others is far more important than blind concentration on practising it ourselves.

The moral perfectionist, and those institutions and organizations which claim to hold the key to moral perfection, tend to discourage others by making them feel that their possible contribution to the realization of a good society is unnecessary, insignificant or unwanted. Hence the reluctance of many to take their share of responsibility in keeping their society's ethical capital intact and growing. They become morally passive and long for a bit of honest home-made evil as a relief from too much overbearing, and probably hypocritical, alien goodness.

Such intolerant and power-backed ethics, that confuses power with ethics and order with goodness, and hypocritically denies individual choice in matters of goodness, may be productive of more social evil than would be found in a society openly ruled by self-interest and instinct. The obvious and eventual answer to the latter is the development of ethical will, but the answer to an imposed monopoly of goodness is return to pre-moral instinct. When rulers believe themselves ethically inspired, and think that no ethics is possible without their rule, they stultify the greater part of society, and succeed in making it appear that whatever is good in the society is due solely to their power, their general benevolence, and their ruthlessness in suppressing 'evil'. They achieve this mainly by suppressing as 'evil' those groups, individuals, institutions and material objects which, if allowed to flourish, would demonstrate that there are as many centres from which goodness can originate as there are centres of consciousness and autonomous will.

The benefits received from another's stock of ethical will

can be paid for, and the other's ethical disposition supported, only in the currency of the benefits received: love is to be answered with love, respect with respect, and generosity with generosity. The payment cannot be in the manner of a restitution or in the spirit with which a debt is paid, nor even in direct reciprocation. Rather it must be in imitation of nature, where trees grow from seed and give seed for future trees. Individuals and groups who do not respond to friendliness and enthusiasms, who are systematically mistrustful and contemptuous of human warmth, are not all exploiters of the ethical capital, for it is doubtful that their disposition allows them to profit from human sympathy and social trust. Their behaviour, however, has discouraging effects, and a society where such people dominate will see its ethical capital dwindle as each of the constituents of that capital circulates with increasing reluctance.

Exploitation of the ethical capital occurs with deep social repercussions when one class or group gains the privilege of behaving in ways forbidden to others and for which others would be punished severely; or when an individual or class or group is exempted from duties or sacrifices which others must perform and are punished if they do not. Exploitation of ethical capital creates false values by injecting into education justifications of the rightness of privileges and exemptions.

Ideally – that is, according to a perfect ethical order and in a perfect anarchist society – there should be no privilege or exemption except when obviously suggested by difference in age, health, intelligence and strength. Equality is a fundamental feature of an ethically inspired society, but respect of diversity is equally fundamental. Differences there will be and must be, and they are marks of exploitation only when those benefiting from them put barriers in the way of others who qualify for similar advantages. Privilege and exemption cannot be justified by pointing to some special sacrifice, a stricter discipline, or a higher measure of restraint on the part of the privileged. Nor can they be justified by some mysterious law of compensation, although the privileged would like the unprivileged to believe that, if they lose in one way, they gain in another and are not worse off than those they envy.

Some inequalities result from the natural movement of ethical impulses towards persons with unusual qualities or particular needs. In identical circumstances, a child is more likely to attract sympathy and be the object of generous and loving attention than an old woman or grown man. Not only in fiction are ladies in distress who find a knight to come to their rescue unusually highborn and beautiful. People outstanding for their contributions or talents gather to themselves a disproportionate share of gratitude and admiration. Differences in esteem, services, homages and gifts received are not fundamentally unethical, although under certain circumstances they may be scandalous and outrageous. A thousand dollars given to a rich film actress by people whose next-door neighbours are starving is a gesture hardly to be commended under any circumstances, but is unjust only if the thousand dollars could have been used to relieve the starvation of the neighbours.

To compare values with one another, and to find a criterion by which to decide their relative importance, is part of the ethical life, and the entrance of power into the decision-procedure or the use of power to correct inequity is destructive of ethical life. Cases of higher or lower ethicality are not all so easy to decide as the one mentioned, and once power is given to enforce one type of ethical behaviour in preference to another there is no drawing a line as to how far this power can be used.

Exceptional deeds, services, qualities or circumstances, which draw to some people an unusual measure of love and admiration, are wont to call forth an unusual measure of envy as well. They excite the greed of the less gifted, less fortunate and less virtuous. Experience shows that reward, especially of esteem, can easily be usurped. Social mechanisms have been devised by which reward is undeservedly secured, cunningly or forcibly exacted, with not even the title, at times of legitimate succession. A king to whom goes the credit for anything good that is done in his kingdom, or a church which claims for her ministers a love and veneration which her founder bought with his blood, are cases of usurpation of reward, which is yet another way of exploiting ethical capital.

The complex of mechanisms by which ethical capital is exploited in modern societies is called the State. The State can be defined as organized exploitation of ethical capital, for such is its main activity and distinguishing feature. A study of the record of States that are no more, and of the structure of those still with us, aimed at assessing how and to what degree each State exploits the ethical capital of the society it fetters, would help protect the ethical capital from exploitation.

Such a study would also serve the cause of truth. Without an understanding of exploitation of the ethical will, the most fantastic and misleading definitions of the State can be given, such as one by a fervent and visionary Russian author that the State is 'organized charity'. Organized charity, which undoubtedly exists, happens not to coincide with the main body of that organization known as the State. On the other hand, if we condemn a particular form of charity because the State has put its seal on it and because we know that this same seal covers the most uncharitable institutions, we are not honouring truth either, for modern States do undertake the organization of charity, sometimes on a large scale. But if this activity is unmistakably ethical it does not follow that the methods used, the persons engaged in it, and the basis of this organization, are likewise ethical. That a potent barbaric chieftain fulfils his conjugal duties to a half dozen wives would be no moral compensation for his having first widowed them all. We have known of heads of State in our time who have claimed filial piety from thousands of children whom they had first ruthlessly orphaned.

Except by usurpation, the nature of the State is not ethical. A wish that the ethical will of a society as a whole should be more powerful than all its particular unethical forces combined is (to take a lenient view) what prompted Idealist philosophers to describe the State as the organ through which the ethical will of a society finds articulation. It may very well be easier to make power ethical than to make ethics powerful, but when ethics comes to terms with power, power dictates and ethics is dictated to.

There is no modern State we can think of that did not originate from an act of violence and usurpation against its own people. Whatever the subsequent ethical history of a State, therefore, no perfectly clear ethical grounds exist on which its acceptance is to be preferred to its violent over-throw. If its foundation is usurpation, its overthrow can be interpreted as an act of just retribution, if not of actual resti-tution, and practically every ethical achievement it may claim to its credit was initiated by people outside its pale, often against its opposition. Only when ethical organizations outside the State are forbidden, and ethical initiative outside the State is punished as a political crime, can one be deceived or frightened into believing that the State is more interested in promoting than in hampering and suppressing the ethical will.

A State differs from other organizations in that it sets no limits to its own extension. That State is most perfect which suffers least competition and has most social activities under its control. Imperialism, however, is not a token of ethics but a characteristic of power. Ethics does not advise the en-slavement or elimination of competitors. A monopoly is always bad, and a monopoly of goodness is worse than a monopoly of evil. The State is an instrument of power, as it shows by sacrificing ethics to power and by exhibiting decay as soon as it lets ethical considerations prevail over counsels of expediency. Only to the extent that its hold on society is lax, and that it accepts criticism and proposals for modification and improvement from people outside its pale, can a State be said to act ethically or for ethical motives. When power to voice criticism and to effect reform belongs exclusively to an organization that, because of its supremacy of power, may be extremely harmful, the ethical w... of society is gagged and bound. The State could be the expression of the will of society only if society controlled the State, and not vice versa. The electoral system pays homage to this principle but in practice is controlled and manipulated by the government in power or by those presumptive governments, political parties.

The State has also been conceived as a force organized for the protection of the ethical capital. That force can be used to protect ethical capital does not mean that the State is force used precisely for this and no other purpose, or that force cannot be used for this purpose outside the State or against it. When the State holds in fact, as it does in intention, a monopoly of force, nothing prevents it from using that force for any end it chooses. Renunciation of force by the majority may allow a minority to take advantage of this renunciation. It is therefore in the interest of those ready to renounce force not to renounce it completely but to be able to count on as much of it as necessary to deter anyone tempted to do them harm. The more precious the material and other goods in their possession, the greater their need of a defender.

But it is not only the peaceful fruits of work and love, not only the ethical capital, that needs guarding and defending. The fruits of looting, slavery and murder need it too, especially if the robbed, the enslaved and the orphaned can muster power. The violent need force for their protection more than the peaceful. It is in the interest of robbers, murderers and exploiters, more than of anybody else, to achieve a monopoly of force, to be surrounded by a disarmed population, and to be able to withstand violent competition.

How much the force represented by each modern State favours the harmless and peace-loving, how much it is at the service of the violent and the parasite, is a matter to be judged separately in each case, but one common feature of all States shows that they are not pre-eminently ethical and that the greatest danger to peace lies precisely in their existence. If it were in the nature of States to be pre-eminently ethical, why so much diffidence and fear between State and State? The more severely so-called crimes against the State are punished, and the more restricted are independent ethical initiatives, the more reason we have to believe that the State is unethically founded.

One more argument brought forward to justify the State is that force is necessary not only to protect ethical achievements but to bring them about. The argument rests on the assumption that the great majority of men are not, and do not particularly want to be, good, and that they must be compelled to it. In its extreme form, the argument affirms that force is the only source of goodness. But he who compels others to be good must be good himself without being compelled. If there is no goodness without compulsion, then the worst specimens of humanity are to be found among those who, administering compulsion, are least exposed to its good effects.

Apart from any question of principle, compulsion is generally resented and its effect on the more intelligent and sensitive is to provoke them to rebellion or to make them work for a day when they in turn will compel others. When compulsion is no longer resented, one may rest assured that spirit has been mortified and that man's capacity for both good and evil has been blunted.

The range of human goodness, furthermore, is vast and any compulsion to goodness must limit itself to promoting a particular kind, to the exclusion and persecution of others – to the exclusion, in particular, of a goodness that considers compulsion an evil and deems ethics in all its positive aspects a matter of choice. Compulsion, as distinct from restraint, must be looked upon with the greatest suspicion because it is so much easier and tempting to compel men to be evil than to be good. Past and existing States, when judged by the standards they apply to individuals, are all guilty of compulsion to immoral acts, and of sapping the foundations of the moral faith of a nation. The claim that murder is no longer murder when done in the service of the State opens the door wide to every evil, for it promises innocence to anybody who alienates his conscience, and any expediency dictated by self-interest is sanctified if only self-interest is clever enough to hide behind the entity, the State, to which conscience is sacrificed.

The rationale of the modern State is to control and direct all social activities, and to weld together every authority and power. It presents itself as a single entity so as to set itself beyond analysis and judgement and to command uncritical submission. This tendency must be opposed, and each service, institution and organization of which the State is compounded must be assessed on its merits. The good or bad of one must not condone or condemn them all. Some see the State as the policeman who directs traffic, others as the troops called in to break a strike, others as the builder of roads and the disposer of garbage, and others as the tax collector, the giver of pensions or the hangman. The State is all these things. The question to be asked is whether each of them is necessary and beneficial to society, not to the State. Would society be better off if this activity were not exercised by the State, or were not exercised at all? Is the price of the upkeep of that activity too great, both materially and in terms of freedom? Are the social benefits of the activity only a pretext for, or completely disproportionate to, the benefits derived by those who control it?

A modern standing army, for example, offers too many substantial advantages to those in charge of it for them to be willing to dissolve it if they were shown that it serves unethical purposes. An army is a necessity for a society surrounded by others with hostile intentions and the means to carry them out. But it is becoming increasingly apparent that societies, as distinct from their respective States, have no hostile intentions against each other. If it is true that a society today cannot dispense with a standing army, and must make it more and more powerful, because other standing armies are also becoming more and more powerful without any being certain of thus diminishing the chances of war, then a momentous step was obviously taken in an unethical direction when the first standing army was created, and the remedy must be sought in the abolition of all armies. A glance over modern European history shows that free institutions and recognition of civil rights developed in those countries where, thanks to natural defences or for some other reason, there was no need for a standing army that could be used by its leaders or the heads of State against the very society it was supposed to protect.

Ethical impulses are erratic and unevenly distributed. Since it is impossible, except in the smallest societies, to synchronize them whenever concerted action is required, organizations are needed to carry out ethical actions whether or not the impulse to perform them is there. Many such organizations are incorporated in the State. When they are developed for their own sake and kept going when their need is past, they are more liability than asset; when ubiquitous and overdeveloped, they drain the ethical capital.

The perfection of such organizations ends by defeating their original intention. Meant to regularize the vagaries of ethical impulse, they finally function automatically and purposelessly, in the absence of ethical impulse. Thus a father may be left with little scope for his paternal zeal when schools and other organizations with large material means provide for his children's needs. A writer will renounce sincerity and lose faith in his message if an organization monopolizes his audience and refuses his work on the grounds that it does not provide the relaxation and excitement that the audience needs.

The services men render to such organizations are greater than the services the organizations render. Because they are machine-like and have the support of all the other organizations comprising the State, they can flout the will of society and ignore its ethical conscience. Perhaps once ethically inspired and ethically conscious, they can now dispense with men who are moved by an ethical will, and make use of men who have a talent for organizing things and keeping them going or for doing what they are told without question. That these two types of men, the organizational and the automatically obedient, should be suitable to a social organ-

ization while others are denied the exercise of an eth
inclined will, is a dehumanizing feature of which no m ii
State is free. These types, which State machines require,
multiply in proportion to the expansion of State machines
and according to the laws (or whims) of supply and demand
in conditions of monopoly or quasi-monopoly. The dehumanization they effect supplies the apologists of the State
with evidence that the State is the only source of ethics, and
that brutishness would be absolute were it not for the State.
People are led to think that society without the State could
not keep together – as if the State had always existed or
compulsion were indispensable, and only slaves could live
peaceably together. But it is enough to say that a State rests
on compulsion, to say that it is unethical.

In order to appreciate the unethical element inherent in
the State one has to compare it not with rival powers it has
supplanted but with what it has replaced in its alleged
sphere of ethical actions. It has replaced habit and customs.
Ethical people, even within the State, make efforts to revive
old customs, to bolster up the few that survive, or to think of
new ones; they seem to realize that customs are the natural
expression of the ethical will of society.

The chief difference between a custom and a State-gener-
ated activity is one of rhythm. The rhythm of custom is, like
biological rhythms, supple, resilient, in harmony with other
rhythms, quickening or slackening its tempo but suffering no
interruption without great risk. The rhythm of a State-gen-
erated activity, on the contrary, suffers breakages and breakdowns and can be repaired almost instantly; it has to be
isolated from other social activities rather than harmonized
with their rhythms; it is altered not so much by change in
the quality of the material with which it works as by change
in the voltage of its engine (the people who give it orders)
and in the number of its cogs and wheels (the people who
obey).

State activities, furthermore, can be scrapped or replaced
without anyone suffering, except by the loss of economic
advantages, privilege and prestige, while customs that are

insulted or prohibited affect people like a wound and share with living tissues the property of growing again. Ethics is originally the same as ethos. Customs die a natural death. State activities, on the contrary, depend on the organizations specifically made for carrying them out, and these are either smashed by the power of another State, disintegrate of themselves under the threat of such power, or are destroyed in a revolutionary explosion. The men in a State machine, as distinguished from those who are its engine, are hired men or slaves. If their place in the machine ceases to mean their bread and butter and personal safety, they care not for its fate as they cared not for its purposes. Although there is no ethics in the absence of caring, the inability of a State organization to win the loyalty of its members augurs well for the future.

Customs and State machines differ very widely in their relationship to education also. Participation in customs requires no special training, except perhaps for an introductory ceremony or period of initiation. Education through custom and to custom teaches people how to live according to the best wisdom of their society and according to what the society values most. But education in a State-controlled society is a process by which a human being is made most useful, or more precisely more usable. The principle is that the best way of being useful to oneself is by being usable by others; and by 'others', of course, one must understand first and foremost the controllers of the State machine.

People will not resent, and hardly be aware of, loss of independence to foreign domination if their customs are respected. Those engaged in keeping customs alive will rise in prestige as they will be looked upon as bravely challenging the customs of the dominating nation. The more that customs are proscribed and persecuted, the more a people will feel that they are turned into slaves. But if the power who wants slaves must destroy the customs of the nation it has subjugated, it need not destroy their State organizations. The conquerer will effect great economies in keeping these intact and in claiming only certain key posts. This in itself

would be sufficient to show that the purpose of State organization is not the good of the people but the good of their
rulers, and that it is an instrument of power and not of
ethics.

The greatest difference between customs and State organizations lies in their attitude towards the past. That of
customs is one of filial piety, matched by parental piety
towards the future. The motive force and goal of customs
can be summed up as perpetuation, which answers to man's
deepest sources of unhappiness and despair – the perspective
of total destruction. There is a soothing, lulling effect in the
regular rhythms of customs, in their alternations and harmonies similar to those of the seasons. A hope of immortality
or of indefinite continuity presides at the birth of a new
custom. New customs arise out of exuberance or immediately in the wake of calamity as the token of ability to survive.

State organizations, on the other hand, are hostile to the
past because it is a natural obstacle to the realization of their
machine-like perfection. To the extent that men owe allegiance to the past they cannot be utilized for the future-
greedy purposes of a *parvenu* State; such men have their
purposes imposed from without. A man is partly his past and
partly his future, and the secret of freedom lies in generating
one's future out of one's past. To rob man of his past is to
make him ready to be the perfect slave. When a State plans
the subjugation of a society that has just fallen under its
power, the first item on its agenda is the liquidation of the
past, understood as a structure of wills, as a system of attachments. By establishing control over productive and service
organizations, the State blackmails society into submission.
It then claims for itself those feelings of gratitude and dependence that each generation owes to all those that went
before; while the only gratitude society owes the State is
that of a slave to his master – the original meaning of the
word 'slave' being a man who has been spared, a man whom
his master chose to keep and not to kill.

The above generalizations obviously do not apply in equal

measure to all existing States. Each of them should, for practical purposes, be studied and judged separately, and the same applies to each State organization and activity. The central idea that we wish to bring forth is the identification of the social with the ethical and of the statal with the unethical and anti-ethical, and this we believe to be demonstrable for every State, from the most to the least totalitarian. A history of the accumulation and exploitation of the ethical capital – its accumulation by society and its exploitation by the State – would be a new kind of history and would throw an entirely new light on political systems.

If activities are judged by the type of man most suitable for carrying them out, government, as the State activity *par excellence*, shows its basic unethicality clearly. For it is not the saint or the compassionate who is wanted in a position of command but the tough, shrewd, unscrupulous man who gets rid of an opposition in one manner or another, who can lie with a straight face, and who is ready to take upon himself the responsibility for any crime necessary to the aggrandizement of the power he commands. Draw a moral portrait of the most outstanding modern rulers – Queen Elizabeth, Peter the Great, Frederick of Prussia, Napoleon, Hitler or Stalin – and try to imagine how, these people being what they were, the machines they built could be ethical in their motives, methods or results. The evils which they are supposed to have prevented are either imaginary or of their own conjuring, while the evils they brought about were very real.

As organizations especially formed for the seizure and holding of government, political parties are unethical too. A party is very much what its name says, a part and not a totality, not the whole of society but a section of it with sectional interests. Parties stand to each other as do nation-states, a permanent threat of ruthless conflict that democratic institutions, if respected, make less costly but also more frequent. Parties are not only the institutionalized expression of the fact that social harmony and peace are not achieved, but are also an open invitation and offer of facilities to anyone who does not want them to be achieved. In each party there are able and ethically inspired people. But they use their abilities and spend their energies mostly in activities and manoeuvres aimed at capturing and holding for their party a position of command. The opinion is justified that if it were not for parties and concentration of political power there would be enough ethical capital about for the whole of mankind to live peacefully and happily together, just as, were it not for economic exploitation for purposes of greed and war, there would be enough wealth produced for everybody to be properly fed and to lead a comfortable life.

The will to reform society, and to bring about conditions of maximum happiness, justice and freedom, has taken on different aspects in the course of history, including that of denying the relevance of ethics when they hinder the attainment of some immediate goal in the interest of the oppressed or, rather, of the political machine allegedly at their service. That the cause of the oppressed should in the latter case turn out to be most unethical and aggressive when ostensibly most successful is not to be wondered at. For to make sure that ethical results are achieved, these must be sought at each successive step, and to make the cause of ethics coincide with the interests of a particular nation or class is unethical to start with and encourages resort to unethical means.

If freedom, happiness and justice are wanted, no slavery must be imposed, no unhappiness caused, and no injustice consummated. If an ethical society is what is wanted, it is the ethical will that must be set in motion, and if an organization is needed, this must serve the ethical will and not a will to power. The ethical will is for the preservation of all that is ethical; what is unethical it must contain and neutralize, always by the least unethical means, and what is not unethical it must leave alone. Finally, when the limits of legitimate self-defence are overstepped, some act of redress or expiation should be performed to avoid confusion of the purposes of ethics with the purposes of survival.

It is of special importance that the votaries of the ethical cause not identify themselves with it to the point of denying the possibility of allegiance to it outside their particular organization. Ethics results from harmony between different seats of initiative; it is a social, never a sectional or sectarian, affair. Ethical capital needs not so much to be created as to be liberated. Thus the mistake and the hopelessness of radical organizations, from an ethical point of view, are that they would have nothing to do with large portions of the extant ethical capital because its exploiters claim to be its depositories and distributors, and because the exploited allow it to be exploited.

If today a radical cause does not appeal to the ethically inspired and disillusionment soon overtakes the ethical activist, it is mainly because radicals and revolutionaries, by their rejection of the extant ethical capital, have put themselves at the great disadvantage of having to create new ethical capital, new ethical wills, new ethical forms, values and names. They have to strain ordinary conceptions, and the new ones they produce are so refined or confused that the great majority cannot understand them or fail to find in themselves anything concrete, alert and living to which they would correspond. The extant ethical capital is not only rejected but left to the exploiters to exploit undisturbed. By denigrating the extant ethical capital and threatening it with destruction, the radicals give reasons to the exploited for accepting exploitation. They make the exploiters appear the true defenders of that capital. The ethical capital is faith, it is what men live by, and men would rather see it exploited than lose it altogether.

Chapter Three **The Ideal**

The realist is defined by his acceptance of the world just as it is, and by his intention to use it to his advantage. He scorns those who (he thinks) waste their time dreaming, whining and grumbling instead of working and fighting for what they want. He endeavours to come out on top always, and if he enjoys success he attributes it to his realism. The realist position would be unassailable if it could be proved that human relationships are all strife and intrigue in which some push upward by trampling others down. But there exists a vast range of activities and relationships that thrives all the better in the absence of strife and intrigue. For people who appreciate such activities, questions of right and wrong, which the realist rejects, are of paramount importance.

The man who enters a race must of course be prepared to puff himself out, and the man who steps into a boxing ring must expect to be punched. But an old sedentary scholar does not expect to be made to run on a track with a pack of mastiffs or a tank behind or to be hoisted into a ring to be used as a punching bag. If either happened to him, he would feel it to be wrong, and if there were disinterested spectators they would share his feeling. The presence of such spectators, actual or possible, is probably what gives him and prompts him to articulate the feeling that there are some things which are and should not be and other things which are not and should be. This feeling is precisely, in its simplest terms, the ethical idealism for which the realist has nothing but scorn. Yet is not the realist an idealist too if, from a position of privilege and power, he affirms that the underdog *should* stay under, that the weak *should not* fight, or that the ignorant *should not* be taught?

That what is now cannot now be otherwise, nobody will deny. But that what is today will be tomorrow, nobody can say. Inertia is not the only force governing human affairs, and change can be and is brought about, so the distinction between things as they are and as they ought to be is a very practical one.

In the world of daydreams the blows delivered by the dreamer inflict pain and death but those he receives, if any, are always slight. Such features of daydreams prompt one to take risks in real life which, without the vision of a world in the shape of one's desire, one would not. Trust in a supernatural power or in constancy of good luck sustains the go-getter, the ambitious and the brave – all those, bar the meek, who possess the earth. Without a streak of irrationality to push him along, the realist would not go far. Though experience teaches him to fit his daydreams to reality, he tackles reality with a view to making it conform to his daydreams, which are his ought-to-be.

If a friend begs us for a loan, and we give it to him and he prospers while we become poor, and when we ask him kindly to return the loan he tells us that we never lent him anything, the shock and hurt we feel are not caused only or chiefly by the monetary loss. If we work in an underground organization, we expect the police to come and seize us at any moment, but we would feel sick at heart if they were guided to our place of hiding by the person who persuaded us to join the underground and whom we trusted as our leader. According to the Gospel, if you ask your father for bread he will not give you scorpions; but supposing he did, you would not only be without bread but without a person you could continue to respect and love as your father. The feeling we experience when we receive evil for good, or fall victim to uncourted and gratuitous evil, is that an order of constancies and correspondences has been broken – an order no less deeply rooted in our mental habits than the order we conceive to exist in inanimate things.

Whatever the motive and purpose of what we consider to be good disposition and good behaviour, we certainly do not cultivate them in order to be repaid with their contrary. To do so we would have to conceive the universe as the work of a sadist and assume that all relationships between persons are sado-masochistic. Harmlessness may meet with violence, meekness with cruelty, trust with betrayal, generosity with ingratitude, and kindness with rudeness. But it does not always happen, and when an association is freely formed or a certain degree of equality obtains we do not expect it. It has happened countless times and happens every day, but before humanity is judged on that score it would be well to compare the record of its wickedness with that of its goodness and to remember that the exception is always more conspicuous than the rule. We would not know of so many evil deeds and evil doers if they had not produced feelings of indignation in other men.

Not to be hampered by moral considerations is, in our present societies and within limits, a condition of success. In special circumstances of wealth and power, moral considerations seem utterly futile, an odd but convenient disposition certain people have to be milked and fleeced. Finally, certain philosophers say that there are no moral judgements, and others say that mankind would go on without them just the same and probably better. The answer is that moral considerations live or perish with faith in an ideal order, to which human behaviour may or may not conform. This order is real to the extent that behaviour conforms to it, and is moral in that behaviour which does not conform to it is felt and judged to be wrong.

Conformity to a moral order may or may not be advantageous to the individual, the group or the species, but to appraise it in terms of usefulness is to submit it to an acid that will dissolve it. Like anything inspired by faith, it is the living acknowledgement of a value, in fact, of a whole set of values.

Values are defined differently by different philosophers but, psychologically, in respect to their role in the mental and affective life of human individuals, they are a body of meanings and attachments. A value is something we care for, and by which we interpret reality and act. The fewer or weaker the values we carry with ourselves, the more meaningless reality appears, the less we care about people and things, even about ourselves.

Ethical values and faith in an order of the ought-to-be not only give meaning to many of our actions and express our concern for other persons, but are also an indication of our care for what may be called the passion of mankind. By our ethical values we preserve the meaning of the numberless ethical actions of past generations and offer a pattern of meaningfulness for the future. Faith in ethical values is that which preserves ethical capital and thereby justifies the faith of all who contribute to it. As long as someone has faith in ethical values, all men who were good, or tried to be good, did not love and struggle and suffer in vain. Conversely, the day when this faith is dead they will all be irrevocably dead, and the realists will be right: it will then be proven that good men are fools.

The idea of moral progress is not necessary to faith in an ethical order. On the contrary it may rob it of some of its strength. The surest guide in moral matters is the feeling that certain actions are good and others bad, whatever the time and circumstances. If cruelty, falseness and cowardice are not evil absolutely, they ought never to be branded as such. Belief in moral progress makes the accident of date of birth more important than the practice of virtue. It may further suggest inevitability and encourage irresponsibility. Most dangerous of all, it tempts one to apply the maxim that the end justifies the means and to eliminate bodily those whom one considers irremediably evil, on the convenient assumption that with them out of the way goodness will develop rapidly and without hindrance.

It can hardly be denied, moreover, that crimes have been committed in our times on a scale and with a perfidy seldom rivalled in the past, and many examples of a good man and a good life to be found in the past are not easily equalled in the present. Good and evil seem not to be functions of evolution. Different forms of social organization encourage particular types of behaviour. People from tribal societies quickly acquire the good and bad ways of Western civilization, while people brought up in this civilization and placed in primitive conditions are caught up by the passions, and seize upon the opportunities for both good and evil, that are particular to primitive conditions.

The theory of moral progress, besides, is associated with the nineteenth-century conception of history as single and uni-linear; the more recent tendency is to distinguish a number of forms of civilization, practically independent of one another, which go through comparable phases of growth, maturity and decay. Because this conception models civilizations after living organisms, it lends itself less readily to the assumption of one standard of morality for society and another for the individual. By suggesting that it is wrong in the infancy of a civilization to live according to values proper to its maturity, or to attempt spiritual rejuvenation when decay has set in, it may still make ethical values time-bound. But one can readily agree that different phases of a civilization are suitable to the cultivation of different virtues and yet hold that what is needed for preservation of faith in ethics is the belief that certain actions are wrong at all times.

To many a modern man, however, thought and behaviour are not fully meaningful unless there is an affective and rational link between mankind today and mankind tomorrow. Man is viewed as an historical animal, sensitive to changes overtaking his species, and as a responsible agent in bringing them about. Whether he cares or not, he will be judged by future generations. There is no escaping the re-sponsibility of leaving certain conditions and not others for generations to come, and this responsibility, accompanied by hope and care for times to come, helps give meaning to the present. But each ethically inspired generation should wish to leave the next generation master of its own destiny, and to limit itself to bequeathing conditions in which, compared with those it inherited, acquisition and preservation of free-dom would be less painful and a choice of tyranny and sla-very more difficult. This it must try to do, although technological advances or breakdowns, new dimensions of the struggle with nature, problems of population, or the unfolding of new human potentialities and concerns, may make the ethical ideal, and essential conditions of freedom and happiness, as we now conceive of them, come to seem irrelevant.

Ethics is not bound to any particular theory, but theories have a bearing upon ethics and cannot be dispensed with if reason and will are to function in harmony. Among the conceptions evolved to understand the nature of ethics, that of 'form' in a quasi-Platonic sense seems to us, although metaphysical, the least likely to offend the commonsense of contemporary biologists. According to this conception the perfectly good man, or the perfect society, is present as a potentiality and trope in every man born and every society formed, more or less as the perfect oak is present in each acorn or the perfect blackbird in each blackbird's egg. Impulses, instinctual or rational, are movements towards explication and fulfilment of a 'form' whose dimension is transspatial and trans-temporal. The form of a perfectly good man or a perfect society, however, is not rigidly the same everywhere but varies from society to society, from individual to individual, and from moment to moment in the life of every society and individual.

By ideal perfection we understand that oak tree that each acorn would realize if placed in those circumstances which are on the whole most favourable. Unfavourable circumstances, such as strong winds, severe cold, insects, fungi and other parasites, especially in the early stages of growth, transform the original ideal of perfection into a succession of ideals of minimal imperfection. So form and life-principle may be considered one, for to say that the organism dies is to say that there is no more ideal form for it to realize. As long as the organism lives (and the same applies to reproductive cells) there is for it an ideal form to realize, whatever change and mutilation it is made to suffer. Imperfect as this form may be when compared with the original, it is perfect as a unity and harmony of parts, which may be more complex than, and in a sense superior to, that of the original.

To use another analogy, in some games of cards there is an initial ideal hand and an ideal course which the game should take in order to secure a maximum score for one of the players. But in each actual game, possible victory for one of the players varies in form and degree with the drawing and playing of each card. When victory, then, is no longer possible, each card that is played, often up to the last, has its own ideal of minimum possible defeat, and it is for the sake of this ideal that the game is worth playing to the last.

So the ideal ethical perfection of one individual or society is not the same as for other individuals and societies, and varies with each change of relevant circumstances and with each ethical or unethical action performed. A perfection that is conceived as lying outside of and unconnected with the ethical agent, unaltered in spite of adverse circumstances and independent of the proportion and manner in which at any given time it is realized, is not an ideal in the sense just explained. In the case of society it is a utopia.

As for every organism of a given species it is possible broadly to define the favourable and the unfavourable circumstances, so it is possible to set forth which general conditions are favourable or unfavourable to ethical life. Ethical life may be exemplified in a great variety of forms but there are forms of life which are unmistakably unethical. If disagreement may be wide concerning what makes life ethical, it is not so wide concerning what makes it unethical. In trying to define the outline of the universal ethical ideal, therefore, it is not only much easier but also far more important to delimit the boundaries of the ought-not-to-be than it is to lay down the rules of the ought-to-be.

The universal ethical ideal has long been known under the name of Natural Law. The present unpopularity of Natural Law among jurists and philosophers stems mainly from their sharing the modern scientific and critical outlook which armours the mind against the awe-inspiring authority of Nature that is found on other counts to be unoperative and therefore non-existent and whose alleged imperatives can be traced to the naïveté and presumptuousness of its champions. It is easy to show that *in* Nature there are no rights but simply relationships of power. A theory of Natural Law based on the totality of Nature would make sense only if Nature were identified with an immanent Mind such as the Stoics suggested. It was under Stoic influence, in point of fact, that Roman jurists set about defining and laying down the claims of Natural Law.

With respect to human affairs, however, Natural Law has no need to postulate a universal Mind; the law will not be that of the cosmos but of man. All Natural Law needs to affirm is that there is a human nature, an entelechy of the living individual, be he typical or singular, and an ability to reason that distinguishes human nature from other natures. The faith sustaining the first efforts towards a theory of Natural Law was prompted by a sympathy for all men; it was a trope toward the root and seed of the unity of mankind.

The student of law will immediately point out that there is no clearly definable general element in human nature of any relevance to law, that there are as many systems of understanding as there are people who understand, and that sympathy, extremely varied in its directions and motivations, can yield the most extraordinary results. There is hardly an action, considered a crime in some society, which some other society has not at some time regarded as legitimate and praiseworthy. Understood as a body of necessary and immutable principles derived from a constancy of human nature and corresponding to a general destiny of man, Natural Law can hardly be defended without appeal to a divine revelation or an extraordinary intuition.

Yet, granting the absurdity of such appeal and taking into account the objections of the relativist, one can preserve unshaken a faith in Natural Law. For if there is no clearly observable and definable general human nature, this may be due solely to the fact that human nature has not yet been fully realized. The conception of Natural Law arose at a time when many nations were brought together. An intelligence that therewith ceased to be linked to national bias and interest saw the inadequacy and invalidity of each particular law. As a matter of political convenience, principles of right and wrong had to be articulated to the satisfaction of a larger and more heterogeneous community than any which systems of law had previously served. As a system of law (and a system of customs, even more so) is effective to the degree that it fits the particular human nature of the community in which it obtains and satisfies their particular conception of the meaning of life, so with the mixing of communities a system had to be devised that fitted a less particular human nature and a less dogmatic conception of the destiny of man. From there, only one further step was necessary in order to conceive the possibility and form of a system of law which would fit a universal community of men.

A theory of Natural Law, therefore, is general to the extent that the system of actual law in which it is incorporated transcends particularities of time and place. Accordingly, Natural Law must not be put on the same plane as historical systems of law. Granted that it cannot lay claim to universal validity; nevertheless it can be rejected only on the basis of principles with a better claim to such validity. Before Natural Law can be criticized on the basis of facts, humankind has first to come together. Until then it should be criticized only on the basis of its rationality and desirability as a possible universal. Conception of this possible universal is indispensable to action and faith centred upon realization of a universal society of men.

To this reinterpretation of the basis and function of Natural Law the realist will object that, among the many theories which may be advanced, that theory of Natural Law will prevail which happens to be endorsed by the power which finally effects the unification of mankind. This power may be a very particular one, and its ideology as far removed from the spirit and tone of the principles most generally held by present partisans of a Natural Law as the spirit and tone of a

Nazi Germany or a Stalinist Russia. But, we answer, if a theory of law is not evolved with a view to reconciling diversities and allowing the co-presence of diverse interests and purposes it is not a Natural Law in the sense we have explained. If an ideology and a system of law are imposed upon mankind by suppressing diversities rather than harmonizing them, then, in spite of its universality of application, it would be only the legalization of a *fait accompli,* that is of brute force. It would suffer from the same lack of rational validity as the historical systems that initially prompted the formulation of a Natural Law.

For the value of Natural Law is precisely this: it attaches no rational validity to a fact simply because it is a fact, and does not recognize a state of things as right simply because it exists. The view of history congenial to Natural Law is not dialectical but generic: it judges the particular through the general, though, of course, intuiting the general through a careful study of the particular. It is interested in the actual but always with an eye to the potential. It looks forward to the future, and through the future it endows both the present and past with meaning.

History is the result of the interplay and the balance, and the upsetting of balance, of forces in conflict. Until reason imposes its own categories, history is as disorderly as nature. Yet reason is seated in nature, specifically in human nature. It is a means of convention of understanding, together with an ideal of what is most fully human. Concerned with human nature, and at the same time its principle of articulation, the ability to reason is not a disincarnate faculty, and if it deals in abstractions it is not in order that the concrete be abolished but to fathom the general so that the particular may be coordinated and understood. When the affective trope that sustains reason is too finely stretched or is broken, we unmistakably sense that reason is becoming inhuman. Natural Law is based on faith in reason; it sees reason as capable fully of containing and finally of bringing to an end the tyranny of force. Reason affords the possibility of solving conflicts without resort to force; it seeks to establish its hegemony, not through centralization of sovereignty, which is the method of force, but by the inverse process of decentralization, by recognizing sovereignty in each human group and individual.

A right established by force takes sovereignty away from where it originally was, and just because established by force it is unnatural in the sense that it breaks an order of things which it is legitimate to call natural on account of its priority. If reason is contrasted with force because it is pacific, any order that is established without force, although it modifies a previously existing order, can still be called natural. The name of Natural Law does not seem after all so inappropriate for a system of rights that does not rest on force.

Natural Law must be complemented by the study and elaboration of social structures most favourable to its realization. From this combination a new discipline, which we may call Social Deontology, is suggested. Its task would be three-fold:

1. To determine what is right and what is wrong in the light of rationality and a comparison of outlooks and experiences, and in a spirit of detachment from contingent interests and ideologies.

2. To solve difficulties and contradictions resulting from the overlapping and apparent incompatibility of principles equally valid in isolation.

3. To suggest forms of organization adhering strictly to principles recognized as right, always on the assumption that it is the general will to see the right principles applied.

This last assumption is of course contrary to fact, and turning it into a fact can only be accompanied by endeavours other than speculation. But a great step will have been achieved to sustain and coordinate these endeavours if faith should be established in the possibility of decisions about right and wrong that are independent of racial, religious, political, economic or personal interests.

If love, honesty and good will could be unchallenged guides of human behaviour, a social deontology would seem unnecessary, and its picture of an ideal society would be only a poor and scanty foreshadowing of the splendour of mankind to be. It is love, honesty and good will that will make and maintain a truly peaceful, just and creative society. But to withstand the destructive impact of their contraries, particularly during their natural lapses, their reality must be kept present to the mind by concepts, and concepts have to be fed and kept alive by concrete or imagined instances. A socially recognized concept of relationships and behaviour is essential for love, good will and honesty to be appreciated, recognized and cultivated. Love, moreover, can be immensely destructive when the form in which it is seen to be capable of realization is made the exclusive historical mission of a particular group and creed.

To devise a set of principles applicable to every society without consideration of historical circumstances would be worse than pretentious. It is neither vain nor vainglorious, however, to give theoretical expression to conditions that must be realized if different societies, different social groups and different individuals are to coexist peacefully. A principle of social deontology, therefore, is validly general in the sense that it is meant to apply to any society, group or individual which, even if it does not make such peaceful accommodation its highest end, is prepared to follow its chosen goals without interfering with others in the pursuit of their goals. General principles of this kind will justify themselves entirely only when applied universally. But lack of universal application does not detract from theoretical validity.

There is no reason why precise definitions and application of inventiveness should not eventually win broad acceptance for a set of principles that would provide a basis for resolving or neutralizing existing disagreements. A charter signed by all people agreeing to end disagreement in all matters of common concern is not likely to remain for long a target for scathing criticism, even if this or that principle is contested bitterly because it is an obstacle to a particular interest or ambition. That an agreement on general principles will be abided by is no more extravagant a hope than any that is presently set, in spite of all misgivings, on this or that written law. General principles are evolved out of consideration of general interests, and it is within the power of man, as a rational animal, to subordinate and sacrifice particular interests to interests that are global and lasting.

One of man's peculiar powers is that of interpreting reality according to his needs and of sometimes attaching more importance to his interpretation than to the needs themselves. Not less peculiar is his ability to combine, enlarge and modify his interpretations of reality and then to demand that reality conform to them. Reality as a rule refuses to conform, but man may still have the last word by interpreting refusal as acceptance. Thus, if among members of a society the same interpretations are believed in, everything happens in that society as if these interpretations were correct. Instances of this come readily to mind in association with reaction, obscurantism and tyranny, but it is to the same ability acting in a revolutionary sense that credit must go for any social and humanitarian progress that was ever consciously achieved.

Wholehearted support of organized violence tends to be limited more and more to a class of professional political, military or commercial leaders who find that they have to reckon with a population more and more critical of politics and leadership, and with their articulate and inarticulate demands for fairness, justice and a minimum of rights. Indeed, though often masked and distorted by loyalty to creeds and endeavours in which they have found support in the past, and though confused and corrupted by expediency and violence, these demands are pretty general, with a claim to universality, and constitute the order of the ought-to-be. A superimposition of this order on the order of being will always be precarious, but precariousness is not the least factor in making many things in life, and life itself, so precious. Awareness of the precariousness of a deontological order should strengthen rather than weaken the determination of each and all to refuse acceptance of things as they are.

The ideal can, in fact, supersede the real if there is a strong enough consensus to act as if the ideal were the real. That 'might is right', for example, is a reality but if the general bias in a community is to consider might as wrong, then the chances of might prevailing over right are greatly reduced. Such truths as 'might is right' or 'a dead man counts no longer' depend mostly on their supine acceptance as truths, based on a finality which applies to physical but not to human facts. Man is, almost by definition, that which is never final and which can choose among different finalities or reject them all.

Two wrongs never make a right but two rights frequently make a wrong. This may be because they happen to coincide with the clashing interests of two parties and to be upheld with a bitterness and blindness that interests alone would fail to inspire. More often it is because particular rights are cherished for themselves, in isolation, and not for the sake of the rightness they all have in common and which, enunciated as a greater right, would show them as separate yet conjoined like branches of the same tree.

The interrelation of all human activities is now so intimate and manifold that nothing short of a global view of a system of principles and their social embodiments can give the historically minded and the realist of politics and economics a sense of the value of ideals. Hence the import of social deontology and the hope of its being welcomed by people who are dissatisfied with both the capitalist and communist systems not because of some accidental and transient imperfections therein, but because they are fundamentally wrong.

The value of an ideal society, as of anything else ideal, does not depend on the greater or lesser likelihood of its realization nor on the nearness or remoteness of the future time when the chances of its realization will be greatest. Rather does it rest on its acting as a touchstone and providing a term of reference and criterion whereby the present forms of society are brought to judgement. So much any conception of an ideal society, apart from a aesthetical appeal or dream-indulgence in legislative authority, springs directly from a need to criticize society as it is.

Every individual has a right to be dissatisfied with the society he lives in. In fact all but a few are dissatisfied with society, though only partly, for varying periods, for different reasons, and with higher or lower emotional force. Whenever dissatisfaction is vented an appeal is made, tacitly or overtly, to an ideal. What distinguishes the realist from the idealist is that the realist appeals to the ideal only as a means of his immediate ends, discarding it as soon as he has made, or failed to make, use of it, while for the idealist the ideal is the end, perhaps never to be reached but always preventing complete allegiance to the real.

If the ideal is not to be a mere excuse and a rational travesty of emotional and unexplored dissatisfactions it must be presented in a clear and coherent picture, avoiding fragmentation, and seeking adherence to the potentially real by a close scrutiny of human limitations, with the least possible reliance on individual imagination. To condemn the real, one should have a clear picture of an ideal alternative, and if this alternative is not rationally satisfactory one should be contented with whatever rationality is always there in the real.

We know as well as the next man that unethical forces are not disposed to relax the grip they have secured on social life by the terror of two world wars and the threat of a third. We know that most men take unethical conditions for granted, and use their natural wits to make the best of them; but rather than accept this as a just cause of despair, we take it as an omen that men will also be able to take for granted and make the best of the best ethical conditions.

It is not that men with ethical zeal and aspirations are wanting or that the part they can play in political affairs is insignificant and ludicrous, but rather that in the absence of clear and uncompromising ethical principles and cautions, and suitable institutions and organizations to attempt their application, they lend their services to those forces that seem to them least unethical, if not in operation then in proclaimed intention. A man of political and mental courage is often lost to the ethical cause because, first, he has before him the example of most men of his kind who have deserted it; second, because these same men, once passed to the opposite camp, kick up clouds of confusion around the ethical cause; and third, because in order to justify apathy or desertion the most suitable temper is to proclaim the ethical cause to be hopeless.

Exploiters of the ethical capital have found it most convenient to perpetrate mass murder and destruction under the conscience-squaring banner of religious or political reform. This has had a ghastly effect on the relationship between people and their languages. The most precious words have been perverted so that their meanings are lost or grievously distorted. One of the main causes of moral and political apathy is this debasement of language. The word 'good', for instance, is often merely the expression of an induced positive attitude, of behaviour conditioned by mass suggestion and backed by real or potential coercion. So a revolution is desperately necessary against the use of a moral language for immoral ends, a revolution prompted by faith in an ethical order and directed against practices that sap all faith in ethical society and ethical man.

Part Two **The Ethical Society**

Chapter Four **Freedom and Authority**

The social machinery

A social machinery is built and kept in running condition to cope adequately, seasonably and economically with ongoing needs and with emergencies that may arise at any moment. It is due to such machinery that a sick man finds a hospital, a doctor, and the medicines he needs. A social machinery can be kept only at the cost of much individual freedom. A doctor has to act as a doctor when he is needed and not only when he feels like being a doctor. Individuals sacrificing their freedom to the discipline of medical practice would not be unjustified, according to the principle of equality, in expecting a similar sacrifice from their patients. An individual or a society may choose between the benefits of a social machinery and the freedom whose sacrifice it requires. But to expect those benefits to be available without sacrifice of freedom is unreasonable and unfair.

A social machinery, on the other hand, may be of such proportions and complexity, and ask for so many sacrifices, as to sound the death-knell of anything that makes life worth living or simply tolerable, especially when it is controlled by people who see in its upkeep the sole or highest purpose of human existence. The cry for freedom is accordingly sometimes the cry for air from individuals stifled by an overdeveloped social machinery, and the reduction of the machinery to simpler forms may be just as salutary and imperative as reduction of desires. An overdeveloped social machinery, besides, serves the interests of tyranny by leaving men fatigued and unavailable for efforts demanded by a new and generous cause. Active lovers of freedom are found most readily among nations whose social machinery is most rudimentary and where much physical coercion is necessary to bring people to heel. The civilized man is hardly aware of losing any freedom by a change of government or the advent of a foreign domination that leaves his social machinery intact or alters it but discreetly.

As a large part of this book is a rational attempt at establishing mechanical constancies over and above the vagaries of life, it can be described as the blueprint of a social machinery. Those who (rightly) associate freedom with the luxuriance of nature will look upon such a project with utmost suspicion. Yet even the most radical of revolutionaries who can think in social and not merely in egocentric or nihilistic terms will know that a social machinery, however simple, cannot with impunity be dispensed with. A social machinery is indispensable when dealing with large numbers of people. But though freedom-limiting it is not identical with political compulsion.

Positive freedom

Positive freedom, animal and god-like, means unimpeded satisfaction of desire. This being so, it is a matter of amazement that freedom could be thought to remain positive when subjected to the condition that it not interfere with the freedom of others. As most of our needs are needs of other persons or demands on their freedom, freedom thus qualified is not worth having. A positive freedom respectful of the freedom of others can be satisfied only through love, through the exercise of generosity and seduction. Otherwise it must withdraw from the social arena and be deployed in the personal or spiritualized social realms of Art, Poetry, Music, Philosophy and Play. In these realms the individual is absolute sovereign. To prescribe in the name of ethics or society how much and what kind of freedom anyone may have in these realms is to extend the violence characteristic of the world of bodies and wills into those worlds that mankind has painstakingly evolved because it is too sensitive and too brave to accept violence as the first and last word.

Negative freedom

The most desirable food from the point of view of the absolute subject, the unhindered satisfaction of desire which we call positive freedom, reveals itself to be a dreadful source of evil when its impact on the subjectivity of other men is taken into account. All things are possible in imagination, and there positive freedom sports and fattens gloriously, guiltless and harmless. But in actuality each event is singular and irreversible, all things are finite, and self-duplication is not possible. Thus in order that the positive freedom of one individual be realized, others are frustrated as his defeated rivals, others are treated like things, as objects of his desires, and others still have their subjectivity twisted and partially paralysed by being used by him as weapons or tools.

From the possibility that every single individual may be a threat to a number of others there arises the conception of a negative freedom, of less but more urgent value than the positive. Animal freedom is wonderful, providing one is a lion and not a gazelle, a stoat and not a rabbit, a cat and not a mouse. More wonderful still is god-like freedom, providing one is a god and not a creature, an emperor and not his subject, a corsair and not his galley-slave. But if one is trampled by competition or turned into somebody else's toy, target or tool, then the wonder of animal and god-like freedom becomes execrable darkness. Negative freedom, therefore – freedom from elimination, objectification and instrumentalization – freedom from harm, is more important than positive freedom, if for no other reason than that it is the latter's vital precondition. As men learn to be less animal-like in the violence and blindness of their appetites, and as the god-like come to look more ridiculous than sublime, negative freedom will summon increasingly wider and lasting support.

Freedom in an anarchist society

Since a life entirely devoid of animal or god-like freedom would be a dull and miserable affair, there are luckily animal and god-like qualities one can cultivate without making oneself a nuisance, and, more important still, without stopping anybody else from cultivating them. The freedom of a Caligula relegates the rest of mankind to a subhuman condition. An anarchist society, whatever positive freedom it may include and foster, cannot include the freedom to be a tyrant. Respectful of autonomous choice among many possible destinies, an anarchist society will exclude many destinies now possible which contain some element of tyranny. The renunciation of satisfaction in tyranny will be more than compensated, to our mind, by the certainty of not having to suffer tyranny from others; though nobody who cherishes tyranny in his heart will share this opinion. We even dare affirm that only people who are not disposed to renounce continual or desultory opportunities for tyranny will oppose in principle a united effort toward the realization of an anarchist society.

In an anarchist society there will be positive freedom, freedom as power, but only in association with others, not over or against them. There is only one way to avoid making the individual powerless against society, and that is a plurality of societies within society, and a plurality of powers within or in accompaniment to each society. This double plurality should provide ample room for each individual to choose from a fair variety of possible destinies. Men agreeing upon fundamental points concerning human destiny, and having similar ideas, tastes, sets of values and styles of life, will naturally unite and share a culture, which is precisely an association to provide the necessary conditions for developing and realizing a particular type of humanity to the exclusion of others. An ethical society, not fully realized until it embraces all mankind, must itself stand apart from culture, while it ensures that each culture within it is tolerant of all others.

For the social thinker who aims both at universality and a plurality of centres of initiative, the concept of freedom must not be endowed with a specific positive meaning but taken simply to refer to conditions of peaceful social living. The freedom with which the ethical idealist and social anarchist ᵒncerned is negative freedom, absence of violence to body

and will, prevention of objectification, instrumentalizati
and victimization of men.

Existential basis of authority

A child's feeling of dependence, even before it is articulated
as filial love, invests the parent with a natural authority, the
authority of authorship, which is the model, though not the
condition, of many other authorities. Feelings of gratitude
and piety on the part of the depending person are most grat-
ifying to the person depended upon. But even when these
feelings are not forthcoming, altruistic behaviour of a parental type is commonly cultivated, partly because it answers
a craving for immortality through transmitting and per-
petuating oneself and partly because, except for the mystic,
human existence is meaningful just to the extent that it is
related to some human being. For these reasons parents
often depend on their children more than their children on
them. The parental role is a continual succession of sacrifices
that shift the centre of psychological gravity out of the self.
Parents find in it a sense of fulfilment not frequently to be
found elsewhere once the various intoxications of youth are
over. Roles modelled on the parental role, by the way, figure
prominently in the dreams from which the more ambitious
of the young derive intoxication.

A life appears completely meaningless when nothing is
felt to depend on it. Not to be the parent, the author and
originator, of anything, is to feel oneself out of place in the
world, completely gratuitous and supernumerary. It is in the
full sense of the word to be unimportant. A man of no importance, a man who does not matter to anyone in any way
may as well never have been born, and may be committed to
death without qualms. Thence the craving in most men for
some form of authority, that is, for recognition of their importance, for justification of their existence. Authority is
more precious than power. There always remains some
power over something, even in the most wretched conditions; there always remains power over oneself, that of

taking one's life away or of not caring if it is taken away; but authority is only over persons and depends on persons; it is that recognition by other men through which a man feels human. It needs constant vigilance and care to preserve, and once lost is difficult to retrieve. Loss of authority leaves a more lasting and bitter taste than loss of wealth and the man without authority is the poorest of men, poorer than the proletarian who has authority over his children.

Authority of authorship

Parents have natural authority over their children in that they are able to provide for the good of their children better than the children can themselves. As long as children remain dependent on their parents for the necessities of life, and for guidance and assistance of any kind, this natural authority is exercised. Similarly the founder of a movement and the initiator of an enterprise have natural authority upon their followers. The latter accept and carry out the decisions because they have not themselves the ability or the courage to make them and yet want them to be carried out.

Power to carry out decisions without the consent of the persons thereby affected is power without authority and is always tyrannical. In order to defend the positive freedom of both the person taking decisions and the person giving him consent, authority needs power to resist any attempt at breaking the relationship on which it rests. The tendency of tyranny to become authoritative by eliminating critics and dissenters, and the tendency of authority to become tyrannical by extending the field of application of its decisions or by abusing consent, are a constant danger to the emergence and balance of associations for the realization of positive freedom.

Authority can now be fully defined as recognized competence within a certain field, and the right to take and carry out decisions with the assent of every person whom the decisions affect. Authority thus defined is not the opposite or the enemy of freedom but its necessary complement. Once it is understood that, in order to be actual in any social sense, freedom is inseparable from authority, nonsensical or deceptive statements about freedom will no longer be made. Authority in fact is the means by which positive freedom can be socially realized without recourse to violence or engendering slavery of any kind.

Ethical authority

Authorship seldom lacks initially all the conditions that make it authoritative but as things develop beyond their origin so the distance increases between the originators and the originated and the competence of the former shrinks together with the latter's willingness to give assent. Authorship and the authority which derives from it are based on love; but ethical authority can dispense with love and must in fact not rely on it, because love may be one-sided or very imperfectly reciprocal and in that case easily becomes tyrannical.

The relationship between any two persons severed from or oblivious of all others is either one of love or one of naked power. Thus an invitation to establish such a relationship is generally feared by the weaker partner, not because love is fearful in itself but because the conditions of love are the same as those of naked power.

Ethical authority arises when a relationship admits of and refers to the presence of a third. To take the simplest case, paternal authority has no ethical meaning whatsoever without the consent of the mother. In fact a tyrannical father is almost by necessity a tyrannical husband. Through sheer superiority of power a father can elicit an expression of assent from his child and a recognition of competence from its mother but that would be a mockery and abuse. Ethical authority, therefore, in order to be genuinely fulfilled, requires that the party granting recognition of competence should be in a position to deny or withhold it without fear.

A son who says that his parents are good educators may be biased by love or fear or may be speaking the truth, but his assertion is not ethically authoritative. An ethically authoritative judgement may, on the other hand, be passed, say, by another parental couple, providing of course that they know all the relevant facts about the behaviour of the first. Recognition on the part of a freely judging third party is what makes an authority ethical. And this is so because the fundamental fact of ethics is responsibility, in the literal sense of having somebody to answer to.

The etymological meaning of 'conscience' is 'knowing together'. To have a conscience is to feel that our actions are judged by other people or, synthetically and supremely, by a personal god. If nobody sees what we do, we may easily persuade ourselves that what we do is right; we may with equal ease persuade others as well if they have only our version to listen to; and of course we have no conscience and do not need one if we are not aware that other men exist who have ability to judge and an interest in what we do.

They have this interest in what we do because they are men like us. The poet who said 'Nihil humanum a me alienum puto' expressed love for mankind, but he also expressed man's right to judge all other men and, conversely, each man's responsibility to all others. 'Do unto others as you would be done by' and 'act in such a way that, if every man acted likewise, only good would result' are maxims devised to bring home vividly to the individual his responsibility to mankind – a responsibility rooted in a similarity and solidarity of fate, subjectivity and intelligence.

When something happens somewhere it may happen anywhere. If we hear of a girl being assaulted and raped, we know that the same may happen to our sister; if we see a mother insulted by her son, we react strongly against it or feel guilty of a similar insult to ours. So also if we hit a child without provocation, for the pleasure of seeng it cry, it is not a matter only between us and that child: our offence is directed against all the children of the world, and we are condemned by any lover of children. If we know beforehand that there are lovers of children, we know also beforehand that our action is unethical. What makes it unethical is precisely the fact that there are lovers of children and that to love children is a widely approved human trait.

Though tending towards universality, ethical judgement proceeds from diversity. The custom of killing slaves so that they may continue to serve their deceased master in an after-life reveals itself unethical by comparison with societies where there are no masters or slaves or where this custom does not obtain recognition. The wider its range of recognition, the more ethical the authority. Width of range is not given by mere spatial or temporal extension but by the number of independent seats of judgement. The principle that everything human is the concern of every man and the principle that human diversity is necessary to the making of ethical judgements stand in real contradiction, and ethical progress is largely a story of their clashing and rubbing together. In an anarchist society this contradiction is solved by leaving every relationship undisturbed with which its contractors are perfectly satisfied, and by rigorously making sure at the same time that there is nothing to prevent them from appealing to a third party in case of dissatisfaction.

Authority and tyranny

Independent power of recognition by a third party provides a criterion by which to decide with certainty at any moment whether the cause of freedom or tyranny is winning ground.

Tyranny is jealous of all authority but its own, and every competence not in its sphere it must either eliminate or make dependent. Tyranny draws all power to itself and wants to be the only source of deliberation and the unchallenged origin of all change. Secret planning and sudden blows, spying and counter-spying, stifling of criticism and suppression of dissenters, are further marks of tyranny, and through them it is self-condemned as consciously illegitimate, alien and hostile to the social whole. In ideologies inspired and dominated by tyranny no intelligent basis is found for law; instead there is the will and whim of the legislator, whose right to legislate has no better foundation than the will and whim of a god made in his image.

Authority on the other hand can only be safeguarded by

being as widely distributed as the modes and nodes of freedoms are numerous and distinct. Authority obtains more widely and is all the better guaranteed the more competent persons there are to exercise it, each commanding recognition of his abilities and approval of their application. In the image of an expanding circle, authority is guaranteed by more authority because it takes a competent person to appraise and recognize the competence of another. Each competence must compete with, limit and be limited by another competence; otherwise it has but little value and can be turned to the destruction of values.

Education has often been rightly perceived and relied on as the best weapon against tyranny, for education is the process by which competent persons come into being. Yet education that is not imparted in a liberal spirit and that lacks the support of integrity is but an instrument of slavery.

By 'integrity' we mean unbroken loyalty to the particular value intrinsic in each competence. The value of weaving is to warm, protect and adorn human bodies; that of bee-keeping to feed people with honey; that of mining coal to provide a source of heat; and so on. A competence is immorally used, and may have serious unethical consequences, when it is used merely as a means to an end, and its intrinsic value is a matter of indifference, ignorance or distaste. It is immoral to learn and practise a job simply as a means to earning one's living. If this is not obvious in the case of production, it hits one in the eye in the social services. The intrinsic value of law is the application of justice; injustice follows straightaway if a judge puts before justice his personal ambition or pecuniary interest. The intrinsic value of teaching is to impart what is believed to be true, and mental warping and discredit of intelligence are the inevitable result of a teaching disrespectful of truth. Loss of integrity, through bribery and corruption or because of compulsion, serves tyranny, not only directly but also in that the authority of any similar competence still exercised with integrity is undermined by an authority or competence to which integrity is no longer attached.

Analysis of leadership

Distinct from and damaging to the principle of authority is the principle of leadership. Leadership is a necessity of war as authority is the fruit and condition of peace. The relationship between leadership and authority in any given society is accordingly the most reliable measure of how much it is at war and how much at peace. Called into being and given power by a state of emergency, leaders must prolong this state or conjure up another, otherwise they are no longer wanted. It is not difficult for any leader thus to retain power when there are other leaders just over the border.

Leadership is destructive of authority because, like love but on a bigger scale, it is a bipolar and not a triangular form of relationship. It excludes and resents observation and judgement; it does not venture into the open spaces of reason but entrenches itself in emotion. It is responsible for the degradation of the individual into the mass-man. Each mass-man, of course, sees himself not as degraded but as a heart and mind in direct contact with the leader's heart and mind, the object and inspiration of his love. He sees and feels all the other mass-men about him as an extension of his body and a multiplication of his power. The bigger and more powerful this body, the more lovable he feels himself in the eyes of the leader, and the more he feels he has something to give him to show his love. But there is no actual love between any mass-man and the others because if there were it would exclude the leader; by making judgement and comparison possible, it would create a situation of freedom and authority.

Authority and freedom, incidentally, are not a negation of love but the necessary condition of its survival when love issues forth in more than one direction and needs to be built into a social system of triangulations. Socially integrated love is inferior to original bipolar love because, starting from the same effective energy, it is of necessity less intense in each of its ramifications.

The mass-man exerts at all times a degrading influence and is potentially murderous because he does not acknowledge subjectivity and authority in anybody but his leader and himself. Others can be lightly or solemnly sacrificed if this is the pleasure of the leader or if it would help the leader to love him better. Theories evolved to rationalize leadership by demonstrating that the individual has no rights and no values are taken by the mass-man to apply to others and never to himself.

The leader for his part does not see the mass of his followers as made up of distinct human beings, but as a composite monster in which the mechanical and the elemental prevail over the human. What makes it at once thrilling and repulsive is its being not only a monster but a monster in love. Though the leader may kindle and abate at will the monster's transports, he cannot escape its grip nor always keep his mind cool when fanned by its animal breath. To the leader the mass is one, none of its parts more valuable than another, all joined in a viscous fluid. It does not matter to him which or how many parts come and go while the monster remains and crouches before him in expectancy and subjection.

In love relationships between two individuals there is a great chance of happiness because they can satisfy their need for each other all the better if they are oblivious of other persons. The relationship between the leader and the mass differs greatly from the normal love relationship in at least one respect. If it is in view of a future child that man and woman are naturally brought together, the many coalesce into a mass and follow a leader in view of the presence of an enemy. In order to keep the bond between leader and led, the presence of an enemy must be constantly felt, and if it does not exist it must be invented. No lovers grow tired of and hateful to each other so soon and so bitterly as the leader and the led if, in the absence of an enemy, they must for a while suffice to each other. When this happens the intelligent leadership always manages to throw upon a new or resuscitated enemy the accumulated anger and self-hatred of the led. In peace, the led are bound to find out their degradation, for it is fear, even if it accompanies predatory urges, that makes them initially accept a leader. When there is no enemy to fear, there is no reason why they should bow to a leader, and if they bow because it is him they fear, then he is their leader only in name and their enemy in fact.

Thus leadership leads inevitably to tyranny as fear takes the place of love. Particular forms of hypocrisy are then established, thanks to which the strongest among the led become nearest to the leader; the nearer they come the more reason they have to fear him and to be feared in turn. The more fear there is the greater becomes the need of mutual reassurance and demonstration of love, until no one is any longer sure of his position or even his own feelings.

The scourge of power

There is one particular kind of ability that is the scourge of every other; the ability to bind other people's will to one's own or else to break it. We use the word 'power' in the sense of concentration and exercise of this ability. While natural authority originates in love and is complemented by love, power strikes fear and carries it within. Power may behave outwardly like tyranny but it differs from it. Tyranny is a usurpation of authority with a view to reaping the fruits of love that are authority's due. Power on the other hand does not believe in love and aims at destroying authority, both natural and ethical. Since it is an ability, power becomes an authority as soon and in proportion as it is recognized. The greatest menace of our times is the authority power is securing for itself in the heart and mind of people, ousting their loyalty to intrinsic values, ousting dignity and desire of ethical achievement. The belief that power is the supreme value, the only worth serving, is obtaining the support of those who by special training and gifts of intellect should be best armed against it. Since both natural and ethical authority belong to a different order and lie as obstacles in the path of power, they are, according to this belief, to be shunned or overrun. A world where power is nowhere hindered except by power seems to satisfy modern minds which, trained in the conceptual clarity of the physical sciences and the simplicity of mechanical facts, find the human world baffling and the human will unwieldy. For them, social and moral considerations only obscure political realities, while the shrewdest among them hold that this is precisely what they are meant to do. Political activity itself consists in finding out which man or combination of men is the strongest; things are right when the strongest is on top; and those who have no courage to fight and are not likely to win must submit or shut up.

The view that competence in the acquisition and use of power is what matters is responsible for social structures and political mechanisms in which those who specialize in this competence take up the task of making history as a profession, decide upon the character and fate of millions, and deal ruthlessly with any intruder.

The surrender of other competences to that of power is dictated by natural cowardice acting on behalf of self-preservation. The greater the sacrifices made for the sake of self-preservation, the greater the accompanying feelings of wrong, resentment and revenge. But while these feelings are alive, surrender is only partial and temporary. So through the State a mechanism and a technique are developed in which surrender becomes permanent and cowardice total.

Whenever the surrender of any competence to another is voluntary, and conducted in the spirit of subordination of a lesser to a more general mood, a contribution is made to the ethical capital. But whenever such a surrender is imposed as the condition of the exercise of any particular competence, and the necessary tools for it lie entirely at the mercy of the specialists in power, we have the most blatant instance of exploitation of the ethical capital.

Authority against power

To prevent the exploitation of the ethical capital and the gelding of men and groups who are repositories of particular beneficent abilities, these men and groups must develop and retain enough power to protect their activities. Ability without power engenders frustration and is responsible for the instrumentalization of values, while the specialization and concentration of power-competence is a cancerous growth within the social organism.

Steps away from the supremacy of power and towards the rule of authority will be: first, dissolving any institutionalized group that specializes in compulsion and is equipped for it; second, breaking down mechanisms such as political parties that promote and give special advantages to the power specialists; third, reclaiming of independence by organizations dominated by the State, and by individuals within State organizations.

As cowardice of some kind and some degree underlies every servitude, so courage is the key to freedom. But true courage is not a free ticket to self-immolation. If there is truth in the maxim that 'No man can be turned into a slave who is not afraid to die', there is equal truth in the dictum that 'A man who runs away lives to fight another day'.

Every competence needs the power to resist all attempts at its destruction or subordination, in other words an antipower that may rely successfully on special techniques but that, in order to triumph, finally requires the solidarity of all who are inspired by the rule of authority and a concerted effort to dismantle instruments of compulsion and prevent power aggrandizement. The power-seeker must be denounced and socially paralysed with the same thoroughness as the freedom-seeker is dealt with in power organizations where insubordination is a crime.

Confusion of authority with power is a common mistake in radical movements. Authority, it needs to be repeated, requires not only competence but consent. Consent is an inclination of the will towards the direction that competence suggests or indicates but never enforces. Power usurps the role of authority by means of compulsion and finally by physical force, so that to give the name of 'spiritual power' to the efficacy of authority against compulsion is not inappropriate. Compulsion and resistance to compulsion are clearly distinguishable even when the latter resorts to force; all one needs to ask is which of the contestants demands more from the other than to be left alone.

Chapter Five **The Rule of Authority**

General conditions

If authority is to reign and tyranny to be kept at bay, the following points may serve as useful guides:

1. Coercive power must be reduced to a minimum and put in as many hands as possible.

2. Claims to authority must be rejected if they are established by force or secured by cunning.

3. All independent centres of authority, while defending their several prerogatives, must be strongly united in solidarity against decisions and actions taken in defiance of the principle of competence and assent.

4. Openness is the mark of intentions that are not antisocial; secret planning and secret organizations, therefore, must never be resorted to and, if discovered, must be unequivocally condemned and rendered powerless.

5. Each authority must be answerable to several others that are equally responsible to several more, in a system that joins all together as in a tangle of chains where each link is interlocked with several others.

It is especially by the last point of multilateral responsibility that our conception of authority differs from the traditional conception of responsibility as unidirectional and hierarchical. A social system stretching fanwise or in a single line places all power in the first link and none in the last. Whenever a link is loose at any end there is either tyranny or slavery. When the whole of society depends on one person, like a swarm of bees attached to their queen, this person is responsible only to himself, which means that he is socially irresponsible. To say that he is responsible to God would be of import only if other men were not also responsible to God, or if he really had the power to take upon himself the sins of his subjects. From the point of view of freedom, both positive and negative, responsibility to the irresponsible is just as tyrannical as irresponsibility itself. Rather than to bind the arms of tyranny, it stretches and multiplies them so that tyranny can do harm more thoroughly and on a wider scale.

Further important considerations are:

1. No person in his relationship with another should be exempt from judgement by a third. This is not to say that every two persons have to give regular accounts to or be spied upon by a third, but that a third should always be approachable for protection and redress if a person is abused or wants to terminate a relationship.

2. Overwhelming power should always be with the third party. This condition is to be ensured by precautions against accumulation of power and centralization of authority, and by unflinching solidarity in upholding the supremacy of the third party, rather than by making a special institution of third-party functions. Any attack against an individual or organization in its judging or mediating capacity should be considered an attack against the whole of society, for the latter consists of individuals who are potentially all third parties.

3. Access to a third party, available to everyone, should be to many third parties, not to one only. Interference with this right of access to one authority after another is an offence against the individual, an attempt to deprive him of the plurality of links by which alone he can be and feel part of society. Such interference is also an offence against society in its most important function, that of protecting its individual members.

4. Contracts between two parties cannot be considered valid. To give them authority a third party is necessary; this party must judge of the fairness of the contract, of its spirit more than of its letter, and of the conditions under which it is signed. This third party's duty and responsibility would also

be to make sure that no outside person is affected injuriously by the terms of a contract.

Elements of competence

A person who is to be invested with authority must not only be competent in the sense of possessing the knowledge and qualifications to exercise authority in the particular field, but competent also in the sense of being directly involved in the activities covering that field. Competence of ability without competence of interest can legitimately act only in an advisory capacity; it may not take decisions but only suggest them, and it may not normally be held responsible for the decisions.

One element of competence tends naturally to be completed by the other: a sick person tries to obtain treatment for his illness while a doctor looks for sick persons to cure. The strongest right of decision rests with the person most directly concerned. A doctor knows which means are most likely to restore a person to health but the person knows whether he wants to be restored to health by those means. Unless there is serious and obvious impairment of vital or rational faculties, pure competence of ability must not prevail over pure competence of interest.

The individual affected (e.g., the patient) must be regarded as the primal and final seat of authority. No interest, and therefore no right, is to be opposed to the interest of a person except the interest of another person or group of persons (e.g. the patient's family, in certain unusual cases). No sacrifice must be imposed upon any person for the sake of hypostatized abstractions such as Society, Freedom or Law, and no offences can be committed against such entities.

An individual is, however, the source and object of affective relationships rather than an isolated physical unit. A mother has competence concerning the health and life of her child. But it is only on grounds of obvious or proven affection and dedication that competence of interest can extend from one individual over another – and never to the extent of annulling his autonomy or paralysing his power of self-determination. Love relationships are all between two persons; there cannot be any question of competence of love on the part of a third. A love relationship is broken, therefore, or at least suspended, when one of the partners appeals to the judgement of a third person. But considering the harm potentially resulting from such a break or suspension, an ethical authority would endeavour to facilitate a perhaps modified resumption of the relationship rather than proceed as if nothing more were at stake than the issue occasioning the appeal.

Knowledge and qualifications give authority only over the field in which they are directly exercised. So for example a supreme educational authority which decides what hundreds of thousands of pupils should learn, although it does not itself teach any of them, is a competence of ability (maybe only presumed) tyrannizing over a competence of interest. Teaching activities have to be coordinated but the teachers and students must have a say in the decisions.

Initial presumption of consent

Society is prior to the individual in the sense that each individual enters society in a condition of utmost dependence that he cannot question or refuse. This fact of unavoidable dependence we regard as the basis for the principle of the 'initial presumption of consent' whereby any individual who is born in a given society is expected to conform to the principles and customs on which that society rests. This principle is ethical if it rests on the care society takes to promote the individual's good, but is unethical when it rests on society's superior power. On the latter basis it was once thought that all persons born in a realm had a duty to bow in all things to the will of their sovereign.

The presumption of initial consent, ethically founded, may itself become tyrannical through the argument that any newcomer owes society a tremendous debt by virtue of the care and attention he receives from the day of his birth to that of his death. Great as this debt is, any newcomer is likely to become a parent himself and to bestow the same care and attention on other newcomers. Whatever cultural heritage the newborn comes into, besides, he comes into through no choice of his own, and he will presumably do his bit for its preservation and enrichment.

The social foundation of ethics is negative and such it must stay. The positive side of ethics must rest with the individual and be his autonomous choice, never enjoined. Products of freedom, gratitude and love are not things that society, or even parents, have a right to demand. The only right that society has over the individual without his explicit approval is that he should renounce force in dealing with other individuals as society renounced the force by which he could easily have been killed when an infant. The renunciation of force is indispensable. The degree of ethicality of any given society is to be measured inversely by the degree of force it exhibits or on which it relies, that is by the number of its murders and executions, of its punishments and compulsions. Compulsions in turn can be measured by the quickness and severity of punishment following attempts to resist or evade them.

Whenever the individual is contrasted with society one must have in mind one particular individual in contrast with all the others. The right of society to presume initial consent is valid only if what the newcomer is presumed to consent to is already in fact consented to by everyone. Thus, for instance, in a society where parents rear their children it is right to condemn the parent who lets his children starve. But in a society where some healthy adults do not work for their living there is *ipso facto* no duty to work. Class distinctions and privileges are therefore unethical. Whether or not they were established and are maintained by force, they invite the use of force to achieve their abolition. Under these conditions even a single individual who rebels against a privilege of birth, or claims that nothing should be demanded of him that is not demanded of others, has right on his side and those who oppose him on this score are acting anti-socially.

Every society owes its existence and particular structure to a very complex mixture of force and its renunciation. Since, however, there is no society apart from the individual members who compose it, every act of force is anti-social and that society is most fully civilized from which the use of force has been excluded. The ethical capital of a society consists in the will of all its members to renounce force. Every act of force asks for retaliation, and most men's lot would be more dreadful than it is if it were not for the fact that most men do not try to live by force. Renunciation of privilege and force, and the turning of inherited advantages originating in force (such as superior education) to the abolition of privileges, are among the chief factors of their ethical progress.

Since one does not usually use force for its own sake but in order to obtain something, it is inconsistent to deny one person the right to use force to obtain what he wants and at the same time to allow another to enjoy what he has obtained by force. An integral pacifist may hold that violence is a worse evil than any of its results, but his cause can hardly be espoused by people in such extremity as to have only violence on which to rely in order to obtain redress. In a society where not everybody is an integral pacifist, initial presumption of consent to the renunciation of force would not be just; one could not expect the presumption to be implemented as long as there are examples of violence which, however strongly condemned, is not denied the enjoyment of its fruits. It is less unethical to use violence to frustrate the enjoyment of violence than it is to encourage its practice by leaving its successful practitioners undisturbed in their advantages.

Inalienability of competence of interest

The fact that no one man can do everything for all others, nor can others do everything for any one man, is a natural barrier to the tyranny of a superman or of an all-provident State. Together with freedom, every man must also share authority and responsibility. In principle each is responsible for all, and without this responsibility no positive freedom that is not anti-social and unethical is possible. In practice, however, responsibility is limited no less than competence and positive freedom.

The inability of a man to attend to all his interests does not make them less his. His sharing of interests with others, his trust in others, and others' trust in him, lead to division and specialization of attention. But the competence of one man in knowledge and performance must not override or destroy the competence in interest of another; nor does one person's habit and capability of attending to particular matters deprive another of a right to attend to them. Freedom, responsibility and sovereignty cannot be separated in principle and must not be alienated in practice. Right of decision, therefore, rests with each individual whether or not he is a member of an association, and the limits of an individual's or an association's sovereignty coincide, not with their power to affect other individuals or associations, but with their likelihood of being affected by the others. However, because of the risks of fallible and imperfect execution, and the fact that actions cannot be revoked, the power of carrying out decisions must rest with competence of ability rather than with competence of interest. It is in everybody's interest to have a house, clothing and food, but not everybody has the ability of a builder, a weaver, a tailor, a farmer or a butcher.

Competence of ability receives final authority from recognition of success. Before the latter is apparent, ability can be tested by judges of tested ability. Trust can easily be abused and come to grief, yet its social value is matchless. To trust the man who has proved to be able is more economical and safer than to trust blindly because one is unable to judge the able. Hence the advantage of a system of competence in the assessment of competence, and of authorities for the recognition of qualifications.

Application of competence of interest

If the principle of competence of interest is accepted, there can be no government but self-government, and if that of competence of ability is accepted, there can be no administration except by experts. Systems of election, delegation and nomination are all to be rejected in principle because they entail alienation of responsibility and freedom, which are recoverable only if the right and power to revoke under any circumstances and at any time are scrupulously maintained. The only system with no alienation of responsibility or injury to freedom is one in which decisions are taken with the participation of all persons concerned and interested; no directives are issued by some to be carried out by others without consent of the latter; persons carrying out decisions affecting others offer the maximum guarantee of competence; no person is prevented from acquiring any particular ability he wants to acquire or from exercising it once acquired.

There is no reason or excuse for government when people are interested in their private affairs, and there is plenty of ability about for the management of social affairs. Apologists of government, defined here as machinery for the passing and enforcement of decisions without consultation with the people who will be affected or the people who will carry them out, are wont to be contemptuous of the standards that the common people follow in private affairs and of their inability to manage their common affairs. These apologists conveniently forget that it is the existence of government that is mostly responsible for the ineptitude and disabilities of the governed.

Everybody likely to be affected by a decision should be consulted thereon, and one should expect no lack of people competent and willing in the management of common affairs. These propositions will hurt the feelings of lovers of privilege, rouse impatience in the idolaters of efficiency, and call for the scorn of the many who assume the impracticability of the yet unpractised. But if a principle is right, ways and means may be found to make it practicable, and the best way of finding them is to try to put the principles into practice. Only thus will it be possible to see what the real difficulties are and what are the causes of failures.

The difficulties attending decisions by vast numbers of

people will be greatly reduced by reducing the quantity of decisions affecting vast numbers; that is, by breaking up centralized social units and returning sovereignty to the smaller authorities from which it was wrenched. Rapid issuance of information to unwieldy numbers is no longer a problem. Methods have been developed, and they can be developed further, that allow vast numbers quickly to make known their will on important issues. Discussion and debate can be carried out by group and intergroup consultations. They can also be greatly simplified by training in the use of words that express one's meanings clearly; by encouragement of intellectual honesty and careful exposition; by discrediting oratorical professionalism and tricks; by abandoning the convention that feelings must be presented under rational garb or that reason that opposes strong or generous feelings must be wickedly motivated. Neutral experts in argument and discussion who sum up the pros and cons objectively before a decision is taken may become a useful institution, although most probably as unpopular as any referee. There should be no shame in stating clearly and simply, when such is indeed the case, that a proposal is accepted or rejected on grounds of personal sympathy or antipathy. It must be recognized that motives and purposes prompting the presentation of arguments are more important than the arguments themselves, and one of the jobs of neutral observers may be to expose and record motives and purposes.

The equitable distribution of sacrifice

The rule of the majority can be as tyrannical as any other. It discourages independent judgement and reduces questions of right and wrong to questions of numbers. That it may be, practically speaking, the least incompatible with freedom within limits of practicality is due to the greater element of revocability which its mechanism contains. There is still room for improving this mechanism, and when decisions by vote are to be taken as a matter of expediency the following suggestions might be considered in order to mitigate or obviate the tyranny of the majority:

1. Whenever possible a solution is to be found whereby majority and minority can each follow their own policy and combine only to avoid clashes and mutual interference.

2. When only one policy can be followed, and the majority is to rule, this must not be interpreted in military terms of victory and defeat but in ethical and pacific terms of 'sacrifice'.

3. For each sacrifice to which a minority is asked to submit a satisfactory compensation should be offered.

4. Or on a principle of equitable distribution of sacrifice, especially when majority and minority are practically constant, every vote, as the expression of a man's will, should go to the satisfaction of that will, proportionately not to the number of men but to the number of acts of will.

To illustrate the last point: if 500 men divided into two groups, one of 300 and the other of 200, are to have 500 decisions carried out, 200 of them should be expressive of the will of the minority. So also for 100 men taking 100 decisions, all of them bar one agreeing each time, it is fair that the 99 should bow to the will of the odd man on one occasion. It is no greater sacrifice of freedom for 99 to do the will of one other once than it is for him on 99 occasions to do the will of 99 other men.

It will be objected that according to this principle of equitable distribution of sacrifice no government is possible. This only goes to prove that government is unethical, not that the equitable distribution of sacrifice is impossible. The objection, of course, will come from those who want to rule, that is from parties and other organizations which, although they call themselves democratic and claim to be mindful of the common good, actually aim at the establishment of their own tyranny. The ludicrousness of the claim that half of a community plus one has the right to dictate its will to the other half minus one becomes even greater when the half plus one is a majority of representatives that does not even correspond to a majority of voters. These and other imperfections and injustices of the electoral and representative system have not prevented the British and American nations from putting up with it for a couple of centuries, or many nations from copying it because they thought it the most ethical and just system. So a system based on the equitable distribution of sacrifice may likewise be given a try.

The main difficulty in the application of the principle of equitable distribution of sacrifice in the form suggested is that neither wills nor policies are quantitatively measurable. Some systems of measuring them, however, may be evolved and agreed upon, and agreement may be reached by replacing a system of rough quantitative measurement by a more sensitive qualitative comparison. Arbitration and negotiations have given satisfactory results on many occasions, and there is no reason to believe that their methods, which ignore the numerical strength of contestants, are not susceptible of more general and perfected application.

An arithmetic of values

The egotistic tendency of every person, usually given as the unavoidable and unsuppressible source of tyranny, can be taken as a basis for defining equality of rights and putting it into practice. Recognition of the subjectivity of others, which marks the dawn of ethics, suggests that in any conflict arising in a common competence of interests rights are equal. That is why such conflicts seem impossible to solve with perfect justice and, unless one party surrenders, are normally solved by ruse, threats, pressure or exercise of force.

A solution is here suggested in the form of an arithmetic of values, to be regarded as a convention which could be accepted by all persons. This acceptance does not seem to us more difficult to arrive at than acceptance of the assumptions and procedure of an electoral system. Varied and elaborate as the development of this arithmetic might have to be as a full-fledged axiological calculus capable of assisting in the solution of complex social problems, its general lines can be stated simply.

Everybody who holds an egotistic viewpoint considers his own values superior to those of anyone else, and if he sees them as transcendental he expects everybody to bow to them as he does himself. Such attitudes are offensive to freedom, to the autonomy of the individual will, and to common reason. Conflicts that do not normally admit of a fair solution are not about means but about values. In the philosophical and religious sphere, each individual association of individuals is free to define and order values according to the truth of a particular revelation or speculation, but from the point of view of peaceful social living, values cannot be considered as transcending the individuals who are asked to live together peacefully, and values are simply the things individuals cherish. If any measurement or comparison is to be made, it will have to be in terms of actual cherishing of things and not in terms of the cherishing that this or that value ought to receive.

A system of social peace is tyrannical and totalitarian if it demands universal acceptance of one system of values. Under a liberal and anarchist dispensation every man must be free to have, and live by, his own system of values. Under this dispensation the ideal solution of a conflict lies in finding the values common to the conflicting parties and in devising a course of action which will satisfy these common interests. But such a solution is seldom possible because it is the values not held in common that generally cause dispute. To overlook them in favour of a common value, even if this value be reason or an ethical principle, may result in an unfair sacrifice of one party to the other, obtained perhaps by rhetorical skill and rationalizing ability.

The idea of an arithmetic of values is not only to make different values of different individuals susceptible of being included in one formula or operation, but also to make sacrifices commensurable with other sacrifices and with compensations and reparations. It may seem absurd to endeavour to devise a method for assessing the value of values and to expect agreement on the validity of this method. Yet there is no more absurdity or extravagance in it than in recognition, in the face of blatant and irremediable individual differences, that all men are equal as regards rights and that respect is due to each. If all men can be, and indeed have been, in legal theory if not in practice, recognized as equal, it is possible and reasonable likewise to recognize each of them as endowed with equal cherishing rights and an equal axiological capital.

It is a principle of social justice that all men doing the same work should receive the same pay, though each will spend it as he individually pleases. In the same way, since all men are members of the same society they should each be credited for the purposes of the arithmetic of values with the same axiological capital expressible in a definite number. This number, equal for each conflicting party, is to be subdivided in as many parts and in such proportions as each party thinks there are cherished things likely to be exposed to sacrifice.

More practical and fairer applications of the concept may be found but here is a method to start from. The two parties concerned, separately or together and with or without the help of a neutral expert, draw a list of all the values or cherished things which they think are affected in the dispute. Each then will distribute his value capital of any arbitrarily selected figure, agreed on for both, among all the desiderata listed, so that the advantages and disadvantages resulting from the solutions proposed by each party can be added up and compared with each other and with the results of any counter-proposal or alternative policy. During the course of one negotiation there can, of course, be no redistribution or *ad hoc* manipulation of either party's quota of value capital, unless agreed upon by both or necessitated because there are too few items to allow equitable give and take.

As an example of conflict to be solved we give a husband and wife who separate and each claims custody of their child. Supposing that the standard value-capital figure is 50, they might each attach 25 'axions' (that is, units of their capital), to keeping the child and 25 to keeping it away from the other parent. At this point no solution is in sight since each parent wants to gain everything and sacrifice nothing. But by both parents' being asked to redistribute their axions so as to cover specific aspects of their wishes, possibilities of compromise and mutual concessions will emerge.

On a more detailed list, then, the axions might be scaled as follows:

Husband's desiderata

Education of the child at a non-religious school	10 ax.
Prevention of mother's destroying child's affection for him	5
Prevention of child's meeting its mother's lover	5
Child's acquisition of habits and tastes from father	10
Father's pleasure in making presents to the child	2
Father's going with the child to and from school	1
Father's having child after school	3
Father's having child weekends	10
Miscellaneous	4

Wife's desiderata

Education of the child by nuns	20 ax.
Keeping child away from father when he is drunk	5
Prevention of father's application of punishment	5
Protection of child from father's corrupting talk	5
Pleasure of looking after child	5
The child's sleeping in mother's house	2
The child's having meals with mother	2
Mother's going with child to and from school	2
Mother's having child weekends	2
Miscellaneous	2

Both lists are such as would be drawn up out of spite and to make sure of winning certain points at the expense of others. They represent, however, a basis for a solution. If the father has the child for weekends (10 ax.), takes it to and from school (1 ax.), and has it for a couple of hours after school (2 ax., reflecting a compromise), is allowed to develop in the child certain tastes (5 ax., again a compromise) and to give it presents (2 ax.), and exacts from the wife an agreement that the child will not meet the wife's lover (5 ax.), the father's gain and sacrifice balance each other exactly. By this arrangement the wife's advantage would be 29 axions (education, care of the child, mealtimes, and sleeping arrangements). Four of these would have to be forfeited or the father's miscellaneous desiderata (4 ax.) be satisfied. In that each would secure as much advantage as was lost, the arrangement would not be unreasonable and might represent the closest possible approximation of equality of advantage and sacrifice. If the father could give satisfactory guarantees that he would never again be drunk in the child's presence and never resort to objectionable forms of punishment, he would bring the total of the mother's advantage to 39 axions and would be in a strong position to propose that the child receive half of its education at a non-religious school.

The principles here suggested (but better ones can certainly be devised) are:

1. An attempt should be made first to satisfy those desiderata presented with the highest number of axions.

2. Unless otherwise agreed upon, the solution should consist in each party obtaining satisfaction of at least as many axions as are sacrificed.

3. As far as possible, each party should have roughly equal advantages and roughly equal losses.

The general principle in whose name an arithmetic of values would be applied is that of the equitable sharing of sacrifice. That, because of the rigidity of any arithmetic, iniquitous use could be made of it should be a spur to finding means of improving it and not a reason for abandoning it in favour of principles that are iniquitous even before their application. It may be, for example, that there is no comparison between the degree of caring for the child of the one and the other parent, and that it is unjust to begin from a premise of equality of rights. But who is going to judge of such things? It might be held that in all questions relating to her child a mother is entitled to greater consideration (i.e., to a greater number of axions) than a father, or that proved drunkenness or adultery should bring analogous adjustments. But such rules would prove far more arbitrary and tyrannical than the dangerous rigidity of the system they would be intended to remedy. As here presented, the arithmetic of values has at least the advantage that each individual is judged, as it were, by his own standards, and each individual case is decided on its own merits. Actual advantages and sacrifices cannot be known; the aim is that each party's conception of his own interest be satisfied. Present-day law does not take into consideration the totality of a situation as viewed by those it affects most, but only those aspects of it that have previously been classified as criminal, illegal, or socially undesirable.

Another example of conflict susceptible of solution by means of the arithmetic of values is that of an economic authority wishing to build a road that would require the demolition of residences. The provision of equivalents of or compensation for each family's sacrifice would be facilitated by ascertainment of the values it believes to be at stake and the relative importance it attaches to each such value. Far more complex, of course, would be an analysis, such as the local authority would require of the economic authority, of the reasons for and advantages to be gained by a particular route; difficult too would be evaluation of alternatives in respect to such factors as the loss of neighbourhood and community relations that residents would suffer. What would be excluded would be any assumption that a roadway represents bigger and more general interests than the interests of the individuals affected and that the former automatically override the latter.

For an arithmetic of values to be applied, there must be only two parties, irrespective of the number of individuals represented in each party. If more than two parties are involved, the dispute would have to be broken into as many bilateral arrangements as the case demands. An arithmetic of values can also successfully be applied in assessment of torts and reparations. Two clear advantages of an arithmetic of values would be: that lying will not pay, as any advantage will go in the direction of stated interests and in the proportion in which they are stated; that ethical considerations will not be used to add weight to, or cover up, interests, since any called in as relevant will absorb numerical strength that would otherwise go to the interests actually at heart.

Authorities in an anarchist society

According to competence of interest there should be local (communal, federal and confederal) authorities, cultural authorities, economic authorities, mixed or mediating authorities; while according to competence of ability there should be juridical, educational and technical authorities. Only the first group need be treated here.

Local authorities

A local authority is a number of people who by the fact of living in a certain area have interests and problems in common. A local authority may in some cases coincide with a cultural authority (e.g., a monastery, a nudist colony) or with one of an economic type, as for instance of people attached to the same factory or receiving their essential goods from the same distribution centre. But its fundamental basis is territorial and its sovereignty does not extend beyond the territory occupied by the population of which it is composed. Local authorities are most necessary where, as in large towns, people of different or unclassified cultures live together.

A local authority's natural concerns would be to ensure that all matters affecting the community were made public and decided upon with public approval; to see that no member of the community was denied freedom of initiative and criticism; to represent and defend the interests of the community and of each of its members in dealing with economic, mediating, cultural and other local authorities; to counteract the power that may be wielded within the community by some section of it (e.g., a professional syndicate, a cultural authority, an emergency corps).

Cultural authorities

People have their religion, their lore, customs, traditions, peculiarities and crazes, and if deprived of them soon tend to develop new ones. Various views on the nature of the universe, various degrees of sensitiveness to mystery, and various decisions as to what matters most give rise to ways of life as precious to the individual as life itself. They are also the true social bond, and without them there is no positive freedom. Historically subordinated to political and economic power, or crushed militarily, they must be given full recognition and chances to develop, though not to proselytize by methods reminiscent of imperialistic, capitalist and colonial abuses, or in any way offensive to the principle of peaceful social living.

The term 'cultural authority' applies to any association primarily concerned with the preservation, development and creation of values. Families, churches, universities, schools of philosophy, literary societies, artists' guilds, sporting associations, clubs, are examples of cultural authorities. Their sovereignty is by nature limited to people who choose to belong to them or happen to be under their tutelage because under age or mentally deficient. They are not to be thought of as coinciding with economic and local authorities unless all persons in a locality or economic unit belong to one of them with not a single exception. Persons in a community who do not feel that they can or ought to give allegiance to any cultural authority might form independent and non-denominational associations with the same status as cultural authorities. Thereby these persons could limit and counteract those activities of cultural bodies which they felt affected them in some unpleasant way, although a check to possible objectionable activities of cultural authorities would always be possible through other authorities, local and juridical.

Whatever the particular aims of a cultural authority might be, its two main functions and conditions for recognition would be: that it should assume responsibility for the behaviour of each of its members acting according to its standards and for all children, if any, trusted to its care; that it provide representatives and specialists (cultural mediators) to settle intercultural differences in a spirit of reasonableness and sympathy.

Economic authorities

Economic authorities are necessary in order that production be coordinated to consumer demand, and distribution be carried out in a just and efficient manner. Together they would form a network of representative boards and committees.

Economic authorities may be producers' authorities or consumers' authorities. In our conception of an anarchist society, workers' authorities (syndicates and trade unions) would be concerned mainly with working conditions, and their dealings would be mainly with 'managements' which represented the consumers' interest within the productive unit (industry, factory, workshop or farm). 'Distributing agencies' would represent the consumers in relation to authorities concerned with planning and coordination.

In an anarchist society the duties of an economic authority cannot be classified as economic work: no position of authority should be sought because of material advantages, and no remuneration should be given. Our conception of the operation of economic authorities is, of course, bound up with our conception of work and wealth in an anarchist society.

Mediating authorities

A mediating authority, in our conception of an anarchist society, results automatically whenever the field of competence of one authority extends over that of another. In principle a mediating authority would consist of all persons whose interests were immediately affected by decisions for such overlapping fields. In practice, competent, voluntary and revocable representatives can be given responsibility for the necessary mediation. Since trade and the coordination of production are rarely confined to a single locality, economic planning necessarily involves such overlapping interests. Such planning would be carried out by mediating authorities consisting of representatives of the persons affected. Again, the revocability of a mandate to represent is a prime article of our conception of a mediating authority.

Chapter Six **Work and Wealth**

Property and usufruct

Man derives his sustenance from the earth, and to the earth
his body returns for the sustenance of other forms of life.
Earth was there before men were on its surface, and it will
presumably still be there when all men have passed away. As
a matter of fact and of right, it is men who belong to the
earth and not vice versa.

If earth does not belong to the human species, even less
can any portion of it belong to any particular group or individual. Soon and irretrievably commingled with its dust, any
man or group of men, be their claims never so loud and so
well supported by force of arguments or arms, will make
room for other men and whatever they build or plunder will
be consumed or taken away.

Reflection upon the shortness of human life and the dis-
solution awaiting all living beings shows both the futility
and the temerity of the notion of property as a sacrosanct
and inviolable right stemming from a natural order of things
and commanding assent from all reasonable beings.

Rights are of two kinds: historical and rational. Indeed,
the notion of right becomes socially operative when the superior and unassailable sanction of reason is asked for a state
of affairs produced by history, or when translation into historical fact is asked for a proposition of reason.

That right is most rational which, less rooted in sectional
interests, is most impartial; that right is most impartial
which is most general, in the sense that its satisfaction is not
hampered or reduced when it is extended to a greater number
of people. Freedom, understood as a set of conditions undisturbed by hostile interference, is because of its very nega-
tiveness the most general of rights.

The right of property could be general to the same extent
if every man possessed exactly the same quantity of the same

things as another, or if the ratio between things desired and things possessed were the same for all. The fact that a man possesses little is in most cases related to the fact that another possesses a lot, just as the positive freedom of a man, what he can do with his will, is in most cases hampered by the positive freedom exercised by another. Like positive freedom, therefore, and precisely for the same reasons, property cannot be claimed to be a general right. In order to be ethical the right must be limited and conditioned. Some other right and some other concept is required to give economics an ethical basis.

A man is the 'owner' of a thing when, thanks to conditions he has grounds to consider durable, he can consume or make use of that thing as he pleases, while others cannot. But as the things his neighbours select for their own use are roughly the same, or soon become the same through envy and curiosity, it is difficult to see how, no other factors intervening, a man can be said to own a thing he does not actually use or consume or why others should refrain from using or consuming it when they want it but do not 'own' it.

The factors that intervene to make the right of property an historical fact are threats of violence against previous users and would-be users, and the forgoing of use of violence by neighbours against the claim of ownership.

Refusal to resort to violence to establish or contest property may be due simply to intelligent fear; it may rest on fables and injunctions in whose authority a whole community, at least ostensibly, believes; it may come from a genuine disinterest in contest and things contested; it may, finally, be the practical conclusion of reason seeking for order in the welter of social facts. It is, in any case, the main staple of the ethical capital of society and the one that has been most exploited and abused.

If property acquired through violence or thanks to unfair competition, slavery or previous spoliation is to be considered lawful, sacrosanct and inviolable, there is no ground for condemning theft or forceful expropriation, because they are exactly the same thing occurring at a different time and affecting different persons.

Every man enters the world completely naked and in every way dependent and parasitical upon the world he enters. Once he is dead – and he can die at any moment – everything the world has given or has allowed him to take goes back to the world and is no longer his. Against this background of impermanence, further accentuated by the power of man to rob and kill his kind, the word 'ownership' becomes meaningless and any claim to property ludicrous and futile.

On the other hand, every man does, while alive, use and consume good things of the earth. He must in fact do so in order to keep alive. He also finds that at least one of his parents provides him with the first things necessary to his life, and that thanks to many other men he can later obtain the necessities, perhaps the luxuries and amenities, of life. So we can speak of usufruct, as we cannot of property, as a clear concept and uncontestable fact, and we can say that whatever a man enjoys is due to the good grace of the earth and of his fellow-creatures who, though perhaps not helping him, still leave him undisturbed when to rob and kill him is in their power.

When a right is invoked, this does not merely mean that assent is asked for an actual or desired state of things; reference is made to a general order, harmony and congruence of things. Without the notion of a general order, of a whole fabric in which no constituent part can be damaged or offended without damage or offence to the whole, the notion of right falls to the ground and there is nothing beyond monadic interests and power to satisfy them, there is no authority to which to appeal, and the hardness and opacity of facts are beginning and end.

The notion of a general order, on the other hand, does not allow the whole to be subordinated to any of its parts or any part to draw advantage from the presence and function of others without contributing something in return. Reciprocity, give and take, are the rule, and in the particular instance of the right of usufruct, enjoyed thanks to the bounty of nature and the good will of men, order and harmony are fulfilled if the good things of the earth are not abused or wantonly destroyed and if the good will of men is reciprocated with equal good will.

The main difference between ownership and usufruct, as rights, is that while the former is irresponsible and unconditioned, the latter is subject to social and economic conditions and carries moral obligations. Whenever, as in many Christian writings, obligations are attached to wealth, the right of usufruct is intimated and that of property implicitly condemned.

Two abiding features of societies based on the right of property are that bodies of men specially trained and equipped for the use of force receive their orders directly or indirectly from the few who possess most riches and that legislation is aimed at protecting and furthering the activities of those few. But a society based on usufruct will require that all its members renounce violence.

The strength of the right of usufruct in an anarchist society will not reside in any special legislation but in the ethical capital of the society, in broad assumptions commonly shared, and in popular sentiment crystallized into usages and customs.

In difficult cases, and whenever claims to usufruct conflict, the problems will be solved by agreement between the interested parties or by judicial appraisal. If the ethical merits of a case are not apparent, or if there should be ethical grounds for incompatible solutions, they will have to be decided by compromise, for resort to force is excluded. So in many instances the terms of a right of usufruct will have to take the form of a contract, subject to readjustment in the light of unforeseen changes of circumstances.

To establish what in particular case constitutes a fair or iniquitous share in the goods of the earth, general principles of ethical economics must be clearly stated, important social facts must be taken into account and analysed, and a system of production and distribution, fundamentally different from capitalism and collectivism, which we condemn as unethical, must be outlined. To this threefold task we now proceed.

Land and natural resources

Uncultivated lands and areas not built up should be for the usufruct of everybody. The fairness of this principle may not be apparent to all, but rejection of it would be tantamount to granting privileges to some and disinheriting others. Whether justice is meant to satisfy needs or merits, a right based on priority of claim cannot be just, even in a society which accepts it, because everything will soon be claimed, to the exclusion of all those who at the time when claims are made are still unborn.

The same principle applies to air, the subsoil, the sea and other waters, providing the use made of them is not dangerous, obstructive, or damaging to others. Air or sea pollution, for example, or aeroplane noises, may be cases for assessment of torts or application of the principle of equitable sacrifice.

For various cultural reasons, and so that man may refresh his feelings for freedom by contact with nature and strengthen his humanity and sense of dignity by watching the cruelties and harmonies of her ways, it is important that as much land as can be spared be not put to use.

Precisely because land is the usufruct of everybody, no one must appropriate any portion either for cultivation or building without the consent of all directly interested in its usufruct. So such allocation would require the approval of the local and economic authorities whose members are most likely to be affected by the use to which the land will be put and by the presence and activities of its user. Approval would be in the nature of a contract in which the competence to grant a right of usufruct is matched by a claim to the right to have it granted. The will of a would-be occupant is in fact likely to be the expression of a vital and crying need, while the opposing interests of local and economic

authorities may often be slight in comparison. Claims to usufruct of land may involve population movements of con-
siderable size, and it is then that mediating authorities, and
adoption of such a system of regulating conflicts as an arithmetic of values, would show their usefulness.

The natural resources of uncultivated lands and waters
(game, fish, firewood, etc.) should, whenever plentiful, be
available for the use of anybody choosing or having to
depend on them. Wilful waste or hoarding would be torts, as
would be deforestation or the wholesale killing of certain
animals or other activities which may seriously upset the
natural economy of a region. The most seriously injured
party is likely to be a future generation. On the same ground
that a father can stand as the injured party when a wrong is
done to his child, associations of persons whose scientific
knowledge is devoted to the welfare of future generations are
entitled to claim reparation for damage to and waste of
natural resources, and to assume responsibility for supplying
necessary information regarding their preservation.

Essential and non-essential goods;
workers and non-workers

It is proposed that all consumer goods and services be
classified into two groups: essential and non-essential.

Essentials comprise those goods and services necessary to
keeping any individual in a healthy and efficient condition.
Essential goods, according to our concept, will be rationed
and distributed free to everybody, that is, not in exchange
for other goods, currency, labour or services.

What is essential should be determined by the individual
himself, a medical authority, and a local economic authority,
jointly. The economic authority might be the same one as
coordinates production and distribution of non-essential
goods, but it could also be one that deals exclusively with
assessing, securing and distributing essentials. As human
needs are basically the same for all individuals, and as the
medical authority is the best judge of special medical requirements, the individual's authority should count mainly

with respect to preferences (e.g., rice instead of bread) and with respect to religious and other cultural peculiarities (e.g., no pork for Mohammedans, no meat for vegetarians).

The supply and distribution of essentials could be organized on lines similar to those adopted in Great Britain and other countries for the supply and distribution of rations during the Second World War. But the concept of what is essential is not limited to foodstuffs. Shelter is an essential. From an economic point of view, hospitals can be regarded as centres of distribution of essential (hygienic) goods and services.

Some people may find it unjust that idle people should be supplied with essential goods free. The idle, however, include the very young, the old, the invalid and the sick. People temporarily out of work through no fault of their own are idle, and so, from an economic standpoint, are those who feel that they can, and would prefer to, devote all their energies, perhaps for an indefinite period, to some unremunerated cultural or ethical pursuit. It is better, in our view, that society provide food and shelter to some economically useless people, such as teachers, priests and so-called social workers, than that it adulterate or impair vocational pursuits by mercenary considerations.

According to the system here suggested, no man is compelled to work. But if he chooses to work he cannot claim all the product of his work, first because he himself, before being capable and willing to work, has been kept alive by the work of others, second because society can claim a compensation for granting the right of usufruct of raw materials and tools, and third, above all, because no mutual trust or kind disposition can be securely established if the foundation of wealth is left an open field for the exercise and gratification of unlimited selfishness.

Only to the extent that it is able through the work of its willing members to mitigate the law of nature which demands effort and ingenuity to obtain the gift of its resources, can a society provide for the needs of its non-working members. Should willingness to work and technical devices both fall so low that not all its members can be supplied with essential goods, nor all its working members with adequate benefit of non-essentials, the able-bodied non-workers will naturally be the first to suffer when a reduction in the individual quota of essential goods is made imperative. The choice of working or starving will then face them, but it would be a choice for which society could not be blamed. Society could no longer be responsible for their keep if it had not enough to keep them. Violence not being permitted, they would have to work in order to live, and by doing so they would help society regain its prosperity on which the generosity of its ethical life depends.

Although the individual should have a say in drawing up the list of his essentials, the criteria to be followed can be general and impersonal because responsibility for supplying them will be generally shared and impersonally fulfilled. Left entirely to extravagant discretion, the choice of essentials would be so varied and extravagant that a society of fairies and genii, not one of producers, would be necessary for its satisfaction. What one person lists as essential to himself would in such a case be scratched out as completely unnecessary by anybody on whom the effort of providing it would fall. The reason is that, psychologically, human beings are eager for luxuries, not necessities. Minimum necessities, objectively assessed, have subjective value only when, owing to scarcity or to difficulty in securing them, they really enter into the category of luxuries. Contrary to general opinion, he is a happy man for whom bread is a luxury, and it is really *les petits bonheurs* which are most genuinely and immensely enjoyed, although man is perhaps more eager for greatness than happiness. By common intelligent consensus, without luxury or the sumptuary quality that necessities acquire, life would hardly be worth living.

Non-essentials, therefore, the luxuries by which life becomes worth living, are also worth the effort to acquire them. Ninety-nine per cent of the truth contained in the interpretation of history called historical materialism is that wars and revolutions begin because people want things that they have gone without for years and sometimes centuries. No war would ever be waged if it were really necessary.

In a liberally and sagaciously organized society, while essentials, by which one merely exists, will be given impersonally and freely, the vast range of non-essentials will be a stimulant of desire that will prompt initiative, sustain effort and direct endeavour, give power of endurance, and make work acceptable and sought after in spite of any unpleasantness it may involve. Work, indeed, in an ethical society, would be the only recognized form of conquest of material non-essential goods. Work will be remunerated in the form of purchasing power, and non-essential goods will be obtainable only through purchase.

No person can be made to work against his will without being thereby turned into a slave. Taken literally, the maxim 'he who does not labour neither shall he eat' is harsh and inhuman. There can be no place for it in an ethical society, for no one is to be deprived of the right to work for somebody else. The Pauline maxim, incidentally, is not applied even in the most rudimentary of societies, and the motherly instinct will not permit strict application of it. As the organization of individuals caring for the general good and its own survival, society must take upon itself the responsibility of ensuring the basic necessities to any person living within it.

As basic necessities are, however, usually the result of some work, if we suppose distribution to be uniform and impartial then the quota obtainable by each person will depend on the total of products available and, therefore, on the amount of work done. Should this total fall below a certain level it will be necessary, in order to raise it again and to prevent the collapse of the whole system by alienating the good will of those engaged in production, gradually to transpose goods from the category of essentials to that of non-essentials. Although in theory, then, the distinction between essentials and non-essentials is relative to the necessities of existence, in practice essentials will be an expression of the degree of productivity and the generosity of a community, while non-essentials will be a stimulus to the production of essentials and a reward for work done.

The standard of living over subsistence level will be in direct proportion to the total work done by the society or community. Obviously this would be so when the system functioned smoothly and prosperously, but it would obtain also in times of scarcity and breakdown, if the principle is applied that the producer has a right to be the first supplied with his product. This principle would have the following results: irrational distribution and waste of transport will be eliminated; distribution will not have the character of confiscation of the worker's product; incentive will be given to communities to work towards a measure of self-sufficiency, greater productivity, and multilateral coordination. A community with no facilities for production of essential goods will have to be in economic coordination with more than one source of their supply.

This principle would put the farm worker at an advantage over the city-dweller. If that seems unfair, far more so would it be if the farm worker were made to work and starve in order to feed the city-dweller. Far from endangering the smooth working and health of the economy, this principle will greatly contribute to it, as a constant reminder of the care which must be exercised in any production planning and movement of labour if there is always to be a more than adequate supply of essential goods. The right of the producer to be supplied first applies only to the minimum indivisible share. Against misrepresentation and possible abuses of this right, such as waste and destruction of products or niggardly productivity, it must be remembered that the right of usufruct can be withheld, or sharing of it required, at any time.

The ethical good will of a community must not be exposed to excessive strain, and the above principle is meant to prevent parasitical communities from arising and striking roots. In a society where compulsion is excluded, agricultural workers will tend to produce only enough for themselves and their families unless non-essential goods are produced for them by other communities. As long as other communities are unwilling to work the land, those who do will be protected against being deprived of their right of usufruct of the land. Hence the necessity for the other communities to produce something to stimulate the productivity of the tillers of the land, and the advantage each community gains by producing as much as possible of what others require in order to have its own requirements for non-essential goods met satisfactorily.

Special ability can replace work and obtain maximum results with minimum expenditure of effort. That is why the acquisition of ability should be considered as much of a social asset as work and should be encouraged by all possible means. The boy or girl who goes to school to acquire a technical ability does so to the advantage of society. The system of remuneration applied to productive work must therefore extend to the training in that ability, and circumstances may require that a proficient student be more highly remunerated than his teacher or than someone in full possession of the ability that the student is only acquiring.

Homes and chattels

As the socio-economic system here envisaged does not recognize the power of buying domestic service, no person or family can rightfully claim usufruct of a house bigger than they need and can adequately look after. Everybody's equal right to a home, on the other hand, does not signify that all homes are to be equal in type, size, number of appliances and so on. In fact, the more that homes are like one another, the less home-like they are likely to be.

Expropriation and redistribution of dwellings may be unavoidable in the transition from an unethical to an ethical society, but it cannot be taken to be a generally satisfactory principle. It would work for only a little time and would call for new expropriations and redistributions as population changes and as new inequalities result from new habits. At each redistribution, besides, feelings of privacy, security and continuity will be frustrated, together with that attachment to one's surroundings that makes a home a richly human and not simply an economic value.

No society would care to guarantee or endorse a right for everybody to the best possible home. The equalization which it would call into being would impose deadly uniformity and relinquish the best for the sake of the best possible for everybody. It would discourage effort towards that which is better, or at least make its attainment a practical impossibility, because every improvement, unless applied everywhere simultaneously, would violate everybody's right to the best.

Another right must therefore be advanced, easier to satisfy, without levelling effects, respectful of human diversity, and bound in its application to prove a permanent incentive to better homes all round. This right can be enunciated as two principles scrupulously to be taken in combination: first, that no one should have a worse home than another; but second, that no one can invoke social justice and fairness in order to get a home as good as his neighbour on the right while his neighbour on the left lives in a worse home than he. So the right to a better home can be exercised only by those living in the worst of homes, and the duty of every local authority would be to see that better ones are made available to them.

There are obvious limits to the pace at which this right can be satisfied, as the number of people with the worst homes will increase as homes get better. These limits will be imposed not only by common sense and by the position of a home in an individual's list of cherished things (chapter 5), but also by the availability of builders and building materials and by what is listed at a given time as essential and nonessential. On the other hand, especially where the building of new houses is in question, it would be sheer stupidity to build them just a little better than those they are meant to replace, not only because it would often be uneconomical but also because it is not fair that the same people always have relatively inferior dwellings. New homes should be provided in preference to sharing or redistributing old ones, and when redistributing or sharing is unavoidable, houses bought under the ethical dispensation as non-essential goods, with the fruits of one's labour, should be the last to be touched, and when touched should be duly compensated for.

Impossible as it is at present to foresee the conditions under which a definite step will be taken in the passage from a prevalently unethical social system to one which makes ethics its prime concern, it seems advisable, in the light of the abuses and blunders of past revolutions, to supplant the right of property by that of usufruct through a gradual re-distribution of dwellings, following the two principles stated above.

The right to a home extends to furniture and other objects that go to the making of a home. The duty of a community is to provide for its members only those objects which are listed as essential goods at any given time. It will be understood that beneficiaries are responsible for the care of accommodations and facilities provided by the community, and that such objects may not be privately bartered or exchanged either for currency or services. Unless dire conditions bring them down to the rank of essential goods subject to emergency redistribution, objects of private amenity or objects made use of in non-economic pursuits may be usufructed undisturbedly and indefinitely.

Farms, pastures, plantations, and any land put to a productive purpose are to be regarded as industrial plant (chapter 7). In countries where there exist strong peasant traditions, however, and the land is the peasant's home, he has a right of usufruct, as the factory worker has to his factory, not only on the principle of competence of ability but also of competence of interest. There can be no compulsion to collectivization or to the formation of cooperatives, which means that even an individual farmer can figure in the economic organization as a productive unit or authority.

Crops can be raised and animals reared for private consumption (not for sale or exchange) providing that there is no pressing consumers' demand for them and that no worker is ready to raise the same crops or rear the same animals to meet the consumers' demand in the established way. Land

and animals, in other words, may within narrow limits and under prosperous circumstances be treated as non-essential goods, as houses can be so treated under similarly prosperous circumstances.

The same rights of usufruct, but no more, are to be acknowledged for cultural authorities as for families and individuals. Only in very extreme circumstances can a cultural authority be asked to sacrifice its right of usufruct for a life purpose. Local and economic authorities are not to use the principle of the primacy of life to do away with cultures they do not like, or to do away with cultural necessities they do not happen to share or understand. For example, a local authority cannot demand that a religious authority sacrifice its place of worship so that it may be used as a hospital when the local authority is not ready to sacrifice a school or other building under its administration to the same purpose. Nor, as another example, may an economic authority demand that a burial ground be turned over to agricultural purposes when it is dearer to the people concerned than their public square or even their houses, and when the needed ground could be obtained by sacrificing a race course or a park.

Chapter Seven Value and Exploitation

The mistake common to most theories of value is that of too intimately relating value to price, to the point even of identifying the two. But the concept of value transcends the realm of economics, even if, as etymology does not suggest, economics was the source of the concept of value. The pre-eminent application of value to economic facts is, precisely, to decide which prices are fair and which unfair. Far from being a purely economic concept, it serves to remind us that economic activities are related to, and never to be isolated from, other human activities.

Price merely expresses the exchange value of an object, and that not genuinely or in every case, because there can be exchange without money and money is something more than a means of making exchange speedier and easier. Money may itself have a price, and sometimes it may have no value.

The professional economist is apt to forget that biological and social needs are often independent of any economic order, and may as easily break such an order as they can be harnessed to pull it along. Needs manifest themselves more naturally and readily in aggressive and predatory behaviour than in the acquisition and expenditure of purchasing power. Nor is aggressive and predatory behaviour exclusively a feature of allegedly primitive societies. Force used to achieve economic ends is a feature of contemporary societies, not only when war is waged but also when a government or similar institution confiscates property or inflicts imprisonment and other pains on those who fail to comply with its requirements (e.g., to purchase a selling licence) or to give up some of their money on demand (e.g., income tax). Disguised as a purely economic or even socially beneficent agency, the coercive apparatus of the modern State sets both the political class of totalitarian countries and the successful capitalists of the democracies apart from the mass of the meek and un-

ambitious, as decidedly as a more open show of force in
another age set a class of barons and squires apart from a
mass of toiling and passive serfs.

An article may change hands without being exchanged for
another; it may be taken away by force and it may be given
away. Shall we say that the article has no value because it is
gotten without payment? Giving and stealing are older than
barter, selling and buying. Their ethical or unethical nature
is also more perfectly clear. Although not usually considered
by the student of economics they must not be ignored by the
student of social facts. The man in the street who cannot
understand all the complexities of the economic transactions
in which he is concerned judges them according to the element of gift or robbery which they seem to him to contain.
He considers him a fool who thinks that all legal instances of
business and all cases in which payment is made are free of
robbery and compulsion, and he suspects him a knave who
would try to persuade him to the contrary. War and taxation
often find their way into the price of things, though they are
not creative of value but are crude acts of depredation.

The ideal exchange, at the back of everybody's mind, is to
get something for nothing. As liberality and spoliation most
nearly fulfil this ideal, the inept will always be inclined to
expect things to fall into their lap, and those well equipped
with physical prowess will always be tempted to resort to
looting and exactions. If true nobility is the best part of
ethics, and if true nobility is the generosity of the strong and
capable towards the weak and incapable, then that society
will be most ethical in which there are most instances of
giving and least of spoliation.

Exchange presupposes property; so all ethical questions
concerning exchange, and each case of exchange ethically
considered, will be decided one way or another according to
whether or not ethical foundations underlie the possession
and disposal of the things exchanged. Leaving the discussion
of these foundations to later treatment, let us concentrate
on how free and ethical is the disposal of property in the
practice of exchange.

The two preliminary requirements of an exchange are that both parties have something to exchange and that both are willing to make the exchange. Normally, the less one possesses the more eager one is for exchange, and the more one possesses the more considerate one is of possible losses and gain and the more leisure and power one has to choose among various possible exchanges. The less urgent one's need, the greater one's bargaining power. Inability to conceal eagerness depreciates the exchange value of the things one is eager to exchange. Ability to conceal eagerness and to affect indifference and even reluctance is one of the commonest tricks to secure the better part of a bargain; but although some are better at it than others, he has stronger cards who can more comfortably do without the exchange.

The exchange value of things, and of money in particular, increases therefore in inverse proportion to their possessors' urgency of need. Competition from others offering the same kind of things, and the presence or absence of similar things on the market, prevents this law from obtaining perfectly but it is discernible enough in common transactions. In countries with a fairly good standard of living, awareness of this law, and hope that it will not be counteracted, contribute to the demand for higher salaries among different trades and professions. That dollar which spreads the possibility of choice over a greater variety of purchasable things, rather than being earmarked for necessary expenses, gives the wage-earner and his wife a greater joy and greater sense of power.

The better bargaining position of a man who has ampler means to satisfy his more urgent needs may be due to parsimony, industry or some other praiseworthy personal traits, but it may also be due to dishonest methods or to a privileged position and training that allow him to profit from legally approved unethical practices. Poverty, on the other hand, may sometimes be due to vice, foolishness or dissipation, but generally speaking people are in such position through no particular fault of their own. They need not be told that it is just their bad luck. Ethical thought and the societal fact itself have no justification if they fail to allay and remedy bad luck.

There is between certain needs a difference of kind rather than of degree, and a similar difference exists between that which must be exchanged in order to satisfy them. A difference of kind exists between needs without whose satisfaction life is no longer possible, and those whose non-satisfaction only makes life a little less comfortable. There is likewise a difference in kind between any article for human use and consumption, and the human person itself, its freedom, its energy and time. To buy labour as if it were a commodity, and to strike a favourable bargain by matching one's secondary needs against the primary needs of another person, are unethical acts because they either effect or assume a dehumanization of man.

The particularly unethical feature of capitalism, also present in managerial societies, is the labour-commanding power of capital. People who, to live, have no legal choice but to hire themselves out as labourers are in no sense free. How well, and even how long, they will live, how much of their life will be spent as they like and how much in a series of acts pre-ordained by others or in repairing the energies consumed by these acts, depends almost entirely on interests that are not theirs. That a mentally and physically capable person should work for his living in a society where other equally capable persons also work may be granted as fair, but that he should not be given opportunity to work, though his work may be socially needed, because it would not be profitable to the detainers of available stocks, is a situation in which no upholder of the capitalist system would like to find himself.

The legalized right of property, and the existence of a propertyless class, the proletariat, who cannot enjoy that right, is but a mitigated, sometimes an exacerbated, form of slavery. Wealth is thereby invested with an extra-subjective value. Without having to use force, and sometimes with hardly any effort, the man who owns a hundred loaves and needs only one is the master of ninety-nine men, and these men, as if not knowing what to do with themselves, will obey his orders and instructions, provide him by their labour with a thousand other loaves, and be thankful for the one loaf he will pay each of them. The capitalist can argue that the thousand loaves would not have been produced without the hundred in the capitalist's possession. But there is no denying the fact that while the hundred loaves had the power to command the workers' labour, the workers' labour had no corresponding power. The unethicality of the situation resides precisely in this unmatched power. The thousand loaves remain in the capitalist's possession, furthermore, so that the situation is perpetuated and there is no global accretion of wealth working for the reduction and disappearance of the propertyless class.

It will rightly be objected that our example oversimplifies and even distorts the actual facts. It serves its purpose, however, because by reference to it any actual relationship of capital to labour can be judged as more or less unethical insofar as it approximates the terms of the example. Additional influences, such as legislation or the strength of capitalist solidarity, as well as the role of the State, can equally be judged as ethical or unethical according to whether they mitigate or enforce those terms.

Exchange theories of value deal with inter-subjective and not with objective value. The objective value of a thing, it seems to us, lies not in its comparison with another but rather in that which makes it comparable – its being what it is, where it is, when it is. Needs, which seem to bestow value on things, can be compared with one another only if things of value are present by which they can be satisfied.

Let us suppose that we are hungry and can obtain a loaf of bread at a nearby shop. The following factors all contributed, although in widely different and perhaps incommensurable proportions, to make the power that loaf has to satisfy our hunger: the services of the shopkeeper and other possible middlemen; the transportation of grain to the mill, flour to the bakery, bread to the shop; the labour, planning, entrepreneurship, organization and inventiveness, thanks to which the means of transport, the bakery, the mill and the agricultural tools and machines were made available for production of the loaf; the labour, knowledge and skill, of bakery, miller, and farmer, that produced the grain, the flour, the bread; the power (wind, water, heat, oil, electricity, etc.) that is harnessed in the mill, the bakery, the agricultural machines and the means of transport; the water, yeast and grain of which the bread is composed and the organic processes that result in yeast and grain; the land that made possible the growth of grain, and the calf's body that made possible the formation of yeast.

In every attempt to found a theory of value independent of exchange, some of these factors are overlooked or misleadingly taken for granted. Labour theories of value take for granted the role of capital and even of entrepreneurship, while pro-capitalist theories take labour for granted; both overlook the primary material and forces Nature supplies. Without taking all these factors into account a theory of value is likely to be more a hindrance than a help in establishing an ethical economic system. In a capitalist system, when costs other than wages have been deducted from income, the remainder becomes a point of contention between workers and employers, the former claiming as much as possible on the strength of their labour, the latter as much as possible in the name of interest, managerial activity, entrepreneurship and new capital investment.

If the price of a finished product available to a consumer is to account fairly for the objective value of the product – for its being available just as it is – all the factors we have listed should be represented. The fundamental ethical objection to capitalism is that into the capitalist's pocket there goes not merely the money translation of those elements of objective value that are mainly put in by him (planning, entrepreneurship, management, organization, investment), but also the money translation of Nature's contribution in the form of power and primary materials, and of the contribution of skills and inventiveness incorporated in the tools, the machines and the very premises needed for production. Even if the workers are paid wages perfectly expressive of the ratio between their labour and the aggregate of all other factors, the capitalist is able to extract a share far larger than is his due.

This unethicality is more apparent in agriculture than in industry, because the landowner may not be responsible for even a fraction of the factors requisite for production. If he inherited the land and delegated its management to an agent, his claims to a portion of the yield of the land can be based only on his letting it out to others. But letting means here, precisely and no more, not being in the way of those who till the land while land, sun and water from the sky play their part with complete disregard for human arrangements. What the landowner claims as his share of the produce of his land, after wages are paid and the cost of implements, seed and fertilizer has been deducted, is really the contribution made by the chemical and organic processes by which seeds develop into plants. Why the benefit resulting from this contribution should go to him, neither the landowner nor any man can explain. The organic and chemical processes accompanying the phenomenon of growth are not of his or any man's effecting. Yet the affirmation and application of the right of property implied that they are. And as the landowner benefits from chemical and organic processes, so the industrial capitalist draws benefits ethically unearned from physical forces and from the ingenuity that discovered the possibility of their utilization and turned it into a fact.

As another approach to understanding value and exploitation we give the following illustrations.

Suppose that following a shipwreck a man perceives a raft, swims to it, and establishes himself on it. Can we say that this man has a right to prevent other swimmers from climbing on the same raft on the ground that he discovered and climbed on it first?

Suppose now that two or three other swimmers succeed in throwing the first man into the sea, and take his place. Can we say that they have a right to decide whether or not to allow other swimmers on the raft, and which to accept, which not to accept, or which to throw back into the sea after first accepting them?

Supporters of private ownership answer Yes to the first question, and supporters of State ownership answer Yes to the second. Not necessarily by their words, of course, but by their deeds.

That, for whatever reasons, including man's nature, things cannot be expected to happen, or simply do not happen, differently, is a matter of opinion or perhaps of fact, but not a basis for ethical judgement. When a right is affirmed, an appeal is made to the ethical sense of man, to his ability and willingness to renounce force, and not to an unethical human nature – still less to an alleged necessity of this nature to accept unquestioningly and irretrievably the finality of a fact.

When one speaks of the first occupant or his dispossessors as having a right to refuse or to allow others on 'his' raft, one does not make a statement of fact (that someone is on the raft and someone else is in the sea) but rather supports a demand that those in the sea should die or be very uncomfortable there if the raft's occupant shows no 'mercy', and should renounce any thought of trying to dislodge the occupant or of forcing him to share the raft.

Rights of this sort, invoked to consecrate the luck or astuteness of a first occupant, or the violence of a second, serve to justify the exploitation of the ethical capital of a community and to intimidate those who are exploited. But such rights cannot be considered as ethically sanctioned.

Imagine now another group of shipwrecked people reaching an island and, casually or by agreement, each establishing himself in a different spot. A drought comes, and there is fresh water in one place only. The man whose right to occupy that place was never disputed would now, according to the capitalist way of thinking, have a right to sell the water to the others or exchange it for their labour as long as they need water. According to communist reasoning, no man has any such right, but the State has. The men on the island who would take it upon themselves to play the role of the State would take possession of the well, share the water out to others in exchange for their labour, and refuse it to anyone who disagreed with the State's methods of distribution, or about the labour imposed in return for the water, or about any other matter whatever.

The ethical solution, by contrast, is that the man on whose ground the well is, allows all others to come and help themselves; they in turn might make a free gift to mark their appreciation of his luck; and they would be obligated to compensate him if they caused him inconvenience or made use of his labour and skill to bring the water to the surface, as they would compensate inconvenience, labour and skill of which they were beneficiaries in other affairs. Should the man not be generously inclined, the others would be justified in helping themselves to the water, and he would be the first to act unethically if he tried to stop them. Especially if it were limited in quantity, distribution of the water might need some degree of control and organization, but such control would be social and not statal, ethical and not tyrannical, if it merely regulated the satisfaction of the need for water, demanded no labour or anything else in return, and excluded no one from its benefit.

In denying the private owner the right to make a profit by selling the water, and the State that of using its distribution as a bargaining counter to achieve purposes other than those which water can serve, we do not only emphasize that a natural resource cannot belong to anyone and that no right or merit attaches to being the first finder or the first finder's successor: we wish also to emphasize the fact, often conveniently obscured but simple and indisputable, that what makes water a commodity or bargaining counter is, first and foremost, the thirst of those who need it. There is no earthly reason why the value of water should be translated into price (money, labour or political submission) and then be taken advantage of by a private owner or State controller, neither of whom plays a part in making the value. If a price is paid for the water, the private owner or the State who profit are not only exploiting the water, which is of no ethical consequence, they are exploiting the needs of men, and that is what makes exploitation unethical. The more vital is the need exploited, the more unethical is the exploitation. And it is monstrously unethical – equivalent to murder – where the need is essential to life.

The ethical terms of the problem do not change when a natural resource other than water is transformed and conjoined with others and transported where needed. Inventiveness, labour, saving and enterprise are then important human additions, and their claim to a reward is ethically justified. This reward should, however, be an expression of social appreciation. It should not be determined by so-called demand, which is expressive of need. Prices in a capitalist economy are an index of the exploitation of needs that things satisfy, not an index of the value of things. Even when the need is secondary or artificially created, there is still exploitation, although more general and difficult to pinpoint, of all the ethical capital and all the labour and organization that created the conditions under which secondary and artificial needs have developed and attracted energies of desire.

There is in the price of *any* article, whether in a capitalist or communist economy, what can be described correctly as a taxation on the needs of the buyer. It is a specious theory that presents profit as a reward for industriousness, risk and enterprise. The inventor, once he has sold his patent, is legally and ethically held to have no rights to any profit his invention may bring to its users. Why is not the entrepreneur and the investor of capital dealt with in the same way? It is clear that once inventiveness, enterprise and possibly a few other factors that go into making and operating a factory have been given a price and paid for, even as wages are paid and a patent sold, any further profit can come only from the raw materials and the labour (including organization and management) which keeps the factory going. The price of labour is represented by wages. When wages, and the cost of raw materials, also made available by labour, and other expenses have been deducted from the sale price of the finished article, no surplus (the profit) can remain that is not the result of sheer exploitation.

This brief analysis has a Marxian ring. We differ from Marx, however, in emphasizing that it is not the worker but the consumer who is exploited wherever profits or, in the case of a communist State, economies are made. Labour as such cannot be exploited. What can be exploited is the man who must work for a price, sell his energy and time, the greatest and best part of his life, because he is a consumer, i.e., a man with a belly to be continually refilled and other needs that in a capitalist or communist economy can be satisfied only if money is first obtained. So the exploitation does not come directly from his employer but from the system of which his employer is a pillar.

What makes wages just or unjust is not the ratio to which they stand to other items in the employer's economy but the amount of necessities they can buy or fail to buy. Although it was reasoned out otherwise by Marxian economics, a worker who is paid one hundred dollars by an employer who makes two hundred dollars profit on his labour is not, and will not feel himself to be, as much exploited as a worker who is paid only twenty dollars by an employer whose profit on his labour is only a dollar or perhaps none at all.

The worker is paid finally by the consumer, and in State-controlled industries wages may be so high as to make it obvious to any unprejudiced observer that the consumers of the products of those industries are exploited by the workers.

The theory that men are exploited as workers came in part from the appalling conditions to which human beings were reduced by the brutal introduction of a system that made labour a commodity, but it came even more importantly from the fact of competition which, before monopolies and quasi-monopolies were established, put a limit on the exploitation of a consumer. It followed that in order to make a profit, the be-all and end-all of his activities, a capitalist had to keep the wages of his men as low as he could, and that the workers had to try to raise their wages as high as they could. Only too commonly in our days, wage claims become an additional factor of first magnitude in exploiting the consumer and in straining a system well nigh to its breaking point.

It has been convenient, because of the increasing complexity of a greatly expanded industry and trade, to identify consumers with workers for purposes of counteracting exploitation. As workers men can strike and exert a significant measure of power. But the aged, the unemployed, the unemployable, who have no labour that can be sold or bought and therefore cannot resort to striking, are not less victims of exploitation, *qua* consumers, than the workers who can strike.

In every system including the capitalist – whether competitive, monopolistic or statal – labour and need, or the production of goods and their consumption, are two different things. Any attempt to measure one by the other is arbitrary and unethical. In State capitalism or communism, of course, exploitation of the consumer is at its worst. Because of lack of competition, the State's power to fix wages and prices and direct consumers' choices, and the abolition of the right to strike, the price of things is entirely out of the consumer's control. His needs count only as long as he is needed as a worker. It is not surprising, therefore, to find in communist countries, though in different forms, the same callousness towards human needs as marked the first and worst days of capitalism.

Only that economy can be ethical – and it will most probably turn out to be sounder than any other economy hitherto – that merely aims at satisfying and not at exploiting human needs.

As a result of capitalist development and industrialization, the earth and its resources are no longer available to the newcomer as they may once have been. Any man born in our century finds practically everything of economic use already claimed and pre-empted for productive purposes. The earth is transformed into a giant factory, and we affirm that this factory is as much the birthright of a man today as it was his ancestor's birthright to conquer and transform the great free spaces of a thinly inhabited and scarcely exploited earth. Coming into being on an industrialized planet brings with it the right to the products of industry, as it did formerly to the natural resources. Family allowances, minimum wages, insurances and old-age pensions are all indications that this right is partially recognized, and that an attempt is being made to superimpose ethics on an unethical system. What is needed for the good, we repeat, of the economy itself is a system based on ethical principles, and such a system must be one in which production is organized for the benefit of the consumer.

In an anarchist society, therefore, industrial plants should be under the joint authority of production units representing the competence of ability of management and workers, and of economic mediators representing the competence of interest of the consumers. This recognition of the consumers' authority over production, together with a method to make it operative, will give a social and ethical sanction to the sound economic principle that consumers' needs (usually referred to as the market) should freely regulate the volume, type and direction of production.

An ethical system aims at rendering impossible the exploitation of any individual, group or class by another. If the right of private or State ownership of plants and producers' goods is replaced by the right of usufruct for those who use them, and if the selling of one's products or services is considered unethical, exploitation should find it difficult to raise its ugly head. Irregularities there might be but, as competence of ability gives the right to participate and check, and as those indulging in irregularities will risk professional disqualification, the total effect could not take the form of regular exploitation.

Management would not be in a position to exploit operatives because it would not be given independent power of remuneration, and might in many cases be unremunerated or less remunerated than the operatives themselves. Management and operatives in conjunction would not be in a position to exploit consumers because the latter would have authority to withdraw the right of usufruct of plants and producers' goods from production units. Wealth, namely currency, supplies or non-essential goods, would be regulated and made available by mediating authorities representing the consumers, so that exploitation could not come from producers.

The danger of exploitation could reside, however, in the power held by these mediating authorities if they were not multiple, mixed, decentralized, with members open to disqualification and displacement. Competence of interest would secure all these conditions, and application of the principle of competence of ability would ensure the maximum of elasticity and control in their composition.

Remuneration of work

In a community of saints, one imagines, everybody would work for everybody else, and would humbly consider himself undeserving of whatever reward, mark of appreciation or gift he would receive. But saints are more concerned with spiritual life than with ethical economics, and in a society where not everybody is a saint, the latter tend to form a class similar to the majority of religious orders both in Europe and Asia that, however charitable and beneficial, are economically parasitical.

More dangerously parasitical, and more likely to develop once methods of coercion are thrown overboard, is the number of people constituting what has been termed society's nursery department. As it is sweeter to receive than to give, and to consume than to produce, not only the beautiful and charming but the lazy and the inept would join the young, the sick and the old to swell the mass of the economically dependent and unproductive.

For these reasons, and because modern complexities of production and distribution do not normally allow the unselfishly inspired to find directly in work the fulfilment and attendant pleasures of giving, it is imperative that remuneration be attached to all kinds of regular services and productive labour.

The object of remuneration is to compensate for the worker's sacrifice of part of his freedom, to give him means to exercise generosity directly and according to his own choice, and to express society's interest in bending selfishness, and acquisitive, competitive and power instincts, towards productive work and regular services.

Remuneration will be ultimately in the form of non-essential goods, but for obvious practical and psychological reasons the use of some form of currency suggests itself, and units of this currency will hereinafter be called *credits*.

In order that different kinds of work be remunerated throughout society according to the same principle of fairness, and so as to stimulate production without offending individual freedom, a new concept must be introduced by means of which it will be possible to find equivalents among widely different types and conditions of work. Amounts of work done, of whatever description, must be made susceptible of measurement and the same unit of measure must be applicable to all types and quantities of work. This unit of measure of work, whose assessment we shall presently explain, will hereinafter be called *ergon*. The rate of remuneration, or number of credits for number of ergons, we shall hereinafter call *edon*, and this measure is to be uniform throughout each community and groups of communities linked into an economic whole by coordinated planning.

It is desirable that the value of the edon and the type of currency adopted should be uniform throughout the whole society. But that might not be convenient or feasible, especially if communities based on the economic principles here suggested arise successively and independently, or if they vary enormously in structure and size.

Measuring work in terms of ergons, and equalizing different kinds of work by relating ergons to edons, is meant primarily to ensure an ethical basis to all economic transactions. But as will be readily perceived its practical applications are hardly less important. Be it sufficient to mention the help it will give to managements in fixing employment guarantees and to trade unions in their assessment of minimum wages, and its overriding role in all financial calculations and planning.

In order to prevent the entrenchment of privileges or sectional claims to preferential or higher remuneration, whether by trade unions or other groups, it is necessary that the number of ergons that an edon remunerates should be as varied and flexible as possible. This flexibility and variability will also prevent the bandying about of spuriously ethical or other specious principles according to which one profession or trade should be paid more than another.

All workers and all work will *not* be paid alike, however. The intention is to prevent injustice, not, as it might superficially appear, to perpetuate it. Supposing all work were paid alike, injustice would result immediately from the allocation of different individuals to more and less irksome jobs. An artificial rigidity would be imposed on the whole economic system with deplorable effects on productivity and the psychology of the workers. Worse still, a system in which economic justice were crudely made to consist in equality of pay could not be established without recourse to coercive measures nor could it be maintained without resorting to them at practically every stage in its career.

The features and factors by which every single productive activity, technical study and service of any kind varies from all the others are innumerable and practically incommensurate. Any objective standard such as usefulness, expenditure of calories, effects on health, etc., will betray subjective bias and will never be able to claim universal assent on rational and ethical grounds. But there is one criterion by which the immense variety of attitudes to varied types of work can be measured if these attitudes are given opportunity freely to express themselves. This criterion is the desirability or undesirability of the various kinds of work made assessable by the number of individuals declaring their willingness to undertake each particular kind.

The system here proposed is to deal out remuneration to each type of work in indirect proportion to its index of desirability. Thus if in a given community, out of 100 workers with a choice between collecting garbage and cutting grass with a power mower, 80 elect the latter and 20 the former, the proportion in terms of desirability between the two jobs is 4 to 1. Supposing the two jobs to be equally necessary, and therefore with the same number of credits to be paid out by their respective managements for their completion, the twenty garbage collectors will each earn four times as much as each of the eighty drivers of power mowers. It is proposed, that is, that while the economic authority in charge of assessing consumer demand may decide which jobs should have priority as most necessary to the life of the community by allocating to different managements different amounts of credits, they have no right to decide which people, how many of them, and by how many ergons per man, will earn those credits.

Within the limits of certain commitments and guarantees aimed at giving workers a sense of security, and at giving managements the minimum of certainty necessary to plan and keep production going, there should be a free movement of labour towards jobs generally considered most desirable. An influx of labour towards them will make them less remunerative, and there will follow an ebb movement away from them towards those previously deemed less desirable but now more attractive on account of the higher remuneration they offer.

One way of initially determining the edon value in credits for each financial year is for the authority in charge of the issuing of credits in a given community or economic unit to divide the total value in credits of the non-essential goods forecast as available for sale within the community or economic unit during the financial year by the number of work-units or ergons forecast to fulfil its production programme in the same year.

The quantity and variety of non-essential goods available for sale (and therefore their global value in credits) will depend on agreements and coordination with other economic units, since it is unlikely that any could be entirely self-sufficient and since a unit would hardly be willing to supply non-essential goods to another unless it obtained essentials or other non-essentials in return. So production ought to be planned in advance of currency issue, though it will itself follow and be based upon assessment of consumers' demands. The global value in credits of non-essential goods available for sale will, then, in the first instance, be arbitrarily established, having regard simply to the easy divisibility of the figure chosen.

Another and probably better way of coordinating production, distribution and currency issue would be to fix the value of the edon arbitrarily, to multiply it by the number of ergons in the productive effort forecast (not forgetting necessary services and technical education), and to use the resulting figure to establish priority claims to supply, after deducting value of goods satisfying the principle of producers-first-served. The same figure would, finally, serve to price non-essential goods, as the total price of non-essentials to be bought in a community during a financial year has to tally with the number of credits issued to the same.

That is, apart from unavoidable imperfections and delays, the non-essential goods made available for purchase by a community will be strictly proportional to the number of ergons that community has put into production, whether of essentials or non-essentials. The same number of edons expressing work done and remunerated will also express the total exchange value (as understood today) of purchasable goods.

The Marxian principle of economic equity will thus be as nearly realized as it has ever been, in that the value of the labour power expended in production will be equivalent to the value of the product created by its expenditure. It will not be fully realized because essential goods will not be put on the market for sale although ergons have gone into their production. To the theoretical and ethical considerations on whose strength this important exception is made, the economic reason may here be added that a system by which everybody is provided with essential goods is the one which will most smoothly ensure a maximum of labour power. Labour power, which consists of muscles, brains, skills and reflexes coordinated to a productive end, is in the case of each man the product of social generosity, because no man ever started earning his living from birth.

If, therefore, a portion of the labour power a man expends does not go back to him in the form of products, he is only paying back to society what society has given him in the first place. He may give society back more than society has given him, but on the other hand he may not. Work in an ethical society must contain generosity. One may choose to be ungenerous, and not work, but he may not choose to work with purely selfish results. Access to and use of the sources of wealth would lead only too easily to exploitation of some form or another, if access to and use of these sources were not left open to all, and if in order to procure the necessities of life some men had no choice but to put themselves at the mercy of others.

Chapter Eight Wrongs and Reparations

Punishment and self-defence

No man has competence, either of ability or interest, to pass final judgement upon another, to decide upon the goodness or badness of another, or to condemn another. There is usurpation of authority, of God's authority, when in a court of law a man is judged for what he is alleged to be rather than for what he has done. There is violence in a court when a man is exhibited as nothing but the author of a despicable action as if, except for one action or a series of actions, often badly understood or misconstrued, his whole life and personality were annihilated.

Evil is a will to do harm. It can be postulated in others but it is known directly and with any certainty only in ourselves. We cannot judge of evil. We can judge of harm and determine from which human agent it has proceeded. To abolish evil may be a pious and praiseworthy desire but we can attempt to do it only in ourselves. The only effective way to abolish it in others is to destroy them. Since destroying a human life is the most evil thing we know of, we should be fair enough to admit the possibility that every evil we wish to destroy is *itself* a will to destroy evil. We can attempt to abolish harm, to remedy and allay it, and to discourage actions which, whatever their intentions, are known to be harmful.

An ethical society takes the standpoint of suffering humanity, not of a humanity that has power to inflict suffering. It favours and draws inspiration from an extension of sensitiveness, not of will. More exactly, it requires an introjection by which other people's sufferings are made our own; it acts from sympathy for those to whom harm has been done, not from loathing for those who caused it. An ethical society, therefore, will have institutions whose specific aim is the relief of harm and the discouragement of harmfulness.

Punishment is the deliberate infliction of pain on a person who has broken a code of behaviour established by somebody else. Its prerequisites are power to inflict pain and its representation of a sequence of events (injunction, disobedience, retribution) as logical and just. A teacher may punish a boy for persistently failing to do his homework but a boy may not punish his teacher, for he knows there will be no social backing for an attempt on his part to give injunctions to his teacher. Having power to inflict pain one can give the most immoral injunctions and have them obeyed; without it, the most moral injunction may be given and it will not be obeyed.

There is no fairness in punishment, first because injunctions are more often than not based on power rather than authority, and second because any correspondence between offence and punishment is bound to be arbitrary, the more obviously when available forms of punishment are limited. As a deliberate infliction of pain, punishment cannot be ethical, and attempts to make it appear so – for example, requiring that it be administered in cold blood, or that judge and executioner not be one – may make it more unethical still. The worst thing about punishment is that, being unethical, it claims exemption from ethical condemnation.

There will, in an ethical society, inevitably be authorized infliction of pain. It must be understood as a defensive measure, not as in any way moral or capable of bringing moral results.

In an ideal society, violence will meet with adequate retaliation because non-violence is a necessary condition for freedom and when violence is committed the condition no longer exists. To let the violent enjoy freedom, and the non-violent lose it at the discretion of the violent, would be stupid, cowardly and unjust. The freedom thus broken cannot be restored except in some cases by forgiveness, repentance and reparation. Prompt intervention, however, can prevent the breach of freedom from extending or becoming a normal state of affairs. In the degree to which a society must use power to check violence and defiance of its pacific institutions, it fails to be a perfectly ethical society.

An act of violence does injury not only to its victim but to those who will have to resort to violence to prevent the violent man from reaping a reward from his violence. This they must do, because where violence pays there can be no faith in freedom. Violence against the violent, however, though perhaps ethical in intention, is unethical in fact. Two wrongs do not make a right, and the containing of violence and the enforcement of authority by power are not expressive of the principles upon which an ethical society aspires wholly to be based. But once the original violent act has broken the ethical order, the biological principle of self-preservation comes to the fore. What is in question is not society's punishment of the violent man but a counterblow by which society defends its freedom, and with its freedom its life.

In an ideal society, by definition, no violence would occur, but an ideal society will never be approximated if measures for making violence unprofitable do not exist. Each person has a right to be defended against violence. Since no one, however, has power sufficient to defend himself against every possible act of violence, and some are likely to invite violence or fall victim to it, an effective power to protect them must be provided.

In the natural order of things an injury asks for retaliation, and in the political order for punishment. While it must reject punishment and retaliation, a society aspiring to be ethical cannot refrain from intervening when injury is done without abdicating its aspiration and without implicitly endorsing an order of violence that is unethical by definition. Its intervention is an act of self-defence and of defence of the ethical order. Without judging an offender except to establish whether and to what extent he suffers from hubris, society will take the necessary steps to avoid repercussions damaging to faith in an ethical society.

Hubris

Hubris is a kind of intoxication or madness, all too easily transformed into a sober system of reason, that leads people to believe, or to act as if they believed, that they have over-stepped the limits of common humanity and that common standards of decency and morality do not apply to them. Some God makes them sacred or some star shields them from error, weakness and infirmities; others exist to bow to and preserve their superiority; a special knowledge is theirs through violence; the weak exist for the strong; and any ethical system, and any force in its service, are crimes against the individual and life.

Hubris is the natural outlook of a vigorous, healthy, inde-pendent and fortunate human animal. Instinctive and ir-rational, it is capable of great intelligence and correct calculations. An anti-social disposition, it assesses people in terms of victory and defeat, and the only way it allows for finding out whether one is right or wrong is by fighting. As long as one is, or hopes to be, successful, one is right; if one suffers defeat and accepts it as part of one's destiny, defeat becomes synonymous with expiation. Hubris is therefore always innocent, and sees itself as responsible only to itself. Because of the great virtue of courage it believes itself to possess, it refuses to see itself as possibly evil.

An ethical society cannot be based on animal aggres-siveness and continual tests of strength. It cannot add its weight to nature and make the helpless more helpless and the strong stronger. Against the truth and order of nature it opposes its own order and truth. For the sake of everyone, of the aggressor himself when brought under control, it will deal with hubris as a dangerous and contagious illness, and he who suffers from hubris may have to be segregated and supervised until declared safely cured.

Persons may be considered to be suffering from hubris when they deny the order of ethical society by refusing to account for their actions when an offended person asks redress, when they are unwilling to make reasonable com-

pensation for their offences, and when they deliberately
evade fulfilment of redress. They can be considered safely
cured when their behaviour shows respect for the ethical
order.

There is a contradiction in describing hubris as an ailment
and in stating that it is a characteristic of the healthy human
animal. Animal health, however, is not ethical health. Although everyone is possessed of hubris at some time or other,
in some degree, no condemnation of human nature follows
from that fact. Hubris is probably as difficult to suppress
completely as is the dramatic sense of life, and perhaps its
complete suppression is undesirable, since it supports that
courage which does not come from despair. In order to overthrow established tyrannical hubris, society may have no
other effective weapon than hubris acting as the mainspring
of rebellion. In times of tyranny the standard of common
humanity is craven submission, and the rebel must, at least
initially, stand apart and above the crowd and trust the
righteousness of his stand to the test of battle.

Tyrants make capital of ethical objections to hubris in
order to strengthen their rule and isolate the rebel, and civilized man degenerates into a tool for the use of the powerful.
Ethical and pseudo-ethical zeal hunts down novelty and
singularity, with the result of a general hypocrisy of mind
and crookedness of heart.

A feeling of superiority or inferiority is probably in-
eradicable from human nature, and ways to excel will always
be sought. What is important ethically is that these ways be
not fraudulent or violent. In its most exalted form, the desire
to excel is identical with God-like freedom and need not be
motivated by hubris. As the conception of God as supreme
power has been modified by other conceptions that present
Him as love, spirit or person, so man's aspiration to be God-
like may seek satisfaction in other ways than the pursuit of
power. Mysticism, asceticism, art, poetry, social and professional dedication, not to mention hobbies and sports, are
so many means of overstepping the limits of common hu-

manity without being socially harmful or ethically objectionable.

Because of the greater danger they constitute, and because they impel society to react with organized violence, collective acts of hubris deserve more serious attention and more severe treatment. The greater the number and power of anti-social gangs, the more imperative the intervention of police forces becomes. A chronic state of gangsterism, political or common, soon dictates its rules to the police and the behaviour of gangsters and policemen becomes indistinguishable. The police become just another gang, and the same type of man – sometimes the same individuals – are found in a police force and in a so-called criminal association.

The basic convictions of collective hubris are that mankind is divided into two classes – the tough and cunning, and the weak and gullible; that if the latter are exploited, robbed and beaten up, it is the natural and just consequence of their having no guts and relying on others instead of themselves; and that the tough and cunning have been created to lord over the others by joining forces instead of cutting each other's throats.

Collective hubris is particularly successful where its tenets are shared by practically the whole of society, and where the weak and gullible accept their lot because each of them believes that he is not quite so weak and gullible as the rest and fails to realize that this belief is precisely what makes him gullible. At the least sign of interest on the part of the strong he thinks that they have recognized him as one of them, and he eagerly anticipates and bends himself to the least of their desires.

Where the mentality of hubris reigns, there can be no ethical society. In an ethical society, education would have the task of seeing that it did not develop. Gangs that resort to violence would have to be met with violence. The stronger they wax, the less ethical the society in which they operate will be. The struggle against them is one for the establishment and preservation of conditions in which ethical life is possible, but it is not itself part of the ethical life.

Law and justice

No society is ethical in which each member does not naturally absorb its governing general principles of right and wrong. Plurality of culture within the same society, with varying standards of behaviour, cannot exclude that respect for other people's ways by which peaceful but diversified social living would alone be possible. Written law represents a generally unsuccessful substitute for a universal understanding of ethical principles.

Written law in most societies suffers from the contradiction that ignorance of law is not admitted as plea, while full knowledge of it can be attained only by a few specialists. It has great difficulty in keeping pace with changing circumstances and with progress in the conception of the nature and conditions of wrong. The letter may kill the spirit; skill in manipulation of its articles may obscure and distort issues and give unfair advantage to the legalistically minded. Although written law may aim at defining unethical behaviour and its punishment so clearly that nobody would dare behave unethically, this intention is commonly frustrated. Shrewd people study the law carefully in order to learn how to behave unethically without violating it, and in the courts the issue is never whether an action is ethical or not but whether it can or cannot be made to correspond to the description for which punishment has been prescribed.

In an anarchist society all distinctions between morality and legality – that is, two standards of right and wrong – should be obliterated. Whereas in archist societies law is generally conceived of as superseding morality in public matters, in anarchist societies judgement of cases would be made in terms of ethical principles alone, except where society sees itself bound to act unethically, i.e., to resort to violence or coercion, against some of its offending and dangerous members. In these latter cases, where we are outside the sphere of the ethical, there would be need for precisely stated regulations to give guidance to those who exert power in the name of society where its authority has failed. Although offending and dangerous members may take advantage of these regulations, a greater risk would be incurred by having people exercise arbitrary power in the name of society and perhaps commit more serious offences than those they are called upon to contain.

To decide what is ethical and what unethical, however, no written law is necessary or helpful.

Every member of a society, from the fact of his benefiting from social advantages, is assumed to be interested in the maintenance of peaceful and equitable social life. This assumption constitutes the ground of the authority of society. When this assumption is contradicted by facts and a wrong is done, an ethical society will need men of experience, sensitive intelligence and keen social vocation to resolve the problems posed. These men, who might be called generically 'assessors of torts', would constitute in an ethical society the equivalent of the basic judiciary in societies organized under political power.

As some of the most tragic cases of violence and offence are prompted by a tortured mind and have an explosive character, a society needs men with good psychological knowledge and experience, whom we may characterize generically as 'preventors', whose primary role is to be available to persons in need of enlightenment, advice and relief. Such persons might be qualified for their position by a special ethical education or by such a vocation as priesthood or psychiatry. They would be considered to be at the service of society in the sense of helping persons surmount difficulties and secure release from potentially dangerous tensions without resorting to violence or causing offence. The reader should not have difficulty in working out the details of how such a system might work; similarly for the functions of 'assessors of torts' and for other procedures that we have merely sketched.

When an offence has been committed, all that an ethically
inspired society can demand is, not that the offender be punished (that is, injured in turn), but that the injured person be
given such satisfaction as to have no reasonable grounds to
feel that he is still injured. Because the responsibility for the
offence is his, and because there is no other way the offender
can assure society that he does not claim the right to do
harm to other people, the burden of compensation falls upon
the offender. When the harm caused by an injury is dispro-
portionately greater than any conceivable intention to harm,
or when adequate reparation is beyond the ability of an
offender, it would be reasonable that third persons be permitted to take upon themselves the burden of reparation;
thereby the offender would not be put beyond the effective
reach of human sympathy and the injured person will have
received compensation.

When an injury is so serious that it cannot be put fully
right, the operative principle should be that the injured
person receive a compensation that entitles him to feel that
he is the object of a beneficent will. On the other hand, the
reparation or compensation asked should never entail a
sacrifice out of proportion to the harm the victim has
suffered, i.e., should never be punitive.

Under no circumstance in an ethical society may the principle of freedom be broken or violence resorted to by any
juridical or enforcement apparatus to an extent greater than
that reached by the acts requiring intervention. The dictum
'que messieurs les assassins commencent' can come only
from a society that looks to its criminals for ethical inspiration.

If both the person who feels himself wronged and the
alleged wrongdoer agree to it, third-party arbitration bind-
ing on both can avert more formal assessment procedures
and is entirely in the spirit of an ethical society. As always, a
main object of such arbitration would be to re-establish harmony whenever it has been broken.

An offender who refuses to accept and carry out a decision
by an ethical authority, whether of 'arbitration' or 'as-

sessment', calls down upon himself the use of compulsion. As well as detention until the offender is willing to annul his offence as arbitration or assessment has prescribed, his voluntary removal to another community, if acceptable to the injured party, may satisfy the defensive needs of the society.

Some form of confinement and compulsory reparation may be necessary in the case of persons committing offences at a rate that threatens to frustrate reparative processes.

Procedures for appeal of decisions must of course be provided. An arbitrated decision may be blatantly wrong or disproportionate, and the arbitrator will thereby be himself an offender whose wrongdoing must be corrected. Where formal assessment of torts is in question, a practical system would be for the local authority to nominate an 'approver' – someone of integrity and competence – to evaluate the assessor's decision, which would not be valid without the approver's acceptance. One can foresee then the desirability of a judiciary chamber, perhaps composed of 'assessors' and 'approvers', whose function would be to reverse or modify unfair assessments, to decide whether assessors and approvers have shown themselves unfit, and to raise the standards of judiciary conduct.

Such are the necessary elements, as we see them, of a judicial system for an ethically inspired society, where the principles of reparation and social self-defence supersede completely the concept of punishment.

Social defence

'Emergency corps' would be a necessity in an ethical society for two main purposes: to cope with destructive natural forces, such as fires, floods and epidemics, and to stave off organized attempts at suppression of liberties. Members of such corps would also naturally be assigned responsibility for detection and apprehension of perpetrators of murders and torts.

The corps and each of their members would be responsible to a judiciary authority for carrying out their functions, and especially for the use of violence that some of these functions may involve.

The ideal is that all the able-bodied men and women in a community who have their freedom and culture at heart should qualify as members of their emergency corps. Nevertheless, although everybody has a right to resist violence and to intervene if it should be inflicted on others, grievous consequences as well as abuses and travesties of this right can be prevented only if people with special training and responsibility are given authority to deal with violence and are called in to deal with it whenever possible and as occasion demands.

The use of violence by emergency corps must be conceived as aiming at containment and frustration of violence, but although this is the negation of something unethical, it is not itself positively ethical.

Any functional equivalent of a police force, militia or army contains the most serious potential hazards to an ethical society, but the need for an emergency corps cannot be evaded. To counteract dangers, it is important that each emergency corps be autonomous, though in touch with neighbouring corps to give or receive help. A centralization of authority is always to be avoided, but most particularly in the case of emergency corps. Their action would have to be counted on to remedy any breakdown in the ethical structure of society. Should any of them use their power to break this structure, society would lie helplessly undefended, unless it were able to count on the fidelity to its ethical principles of all or most of the others.

In order further to minimize the possibility of degeneration of a system of emergency corps, procedures on the following order would be desirable: complete separation of emergency corps from cultural organizations; requirement of judicial approval for all non-routine emergency corps activities; frequent rotation of members; non-remuneration of services; individual accountability.

Without discipline an emergency corps would in many cases prove ineffective and thus not justify its existence. To become a member of one would therefore be a serious commitment, as it would imply temporary if partial alienation of freedom and, above all, carrying out acts repellent to a sensitive ethical conscience. A member would have to be considered personally responsible for any instructions he carried out, quite as much as the persons issuing the instructions. He would therefore be fully within his right, and ethically obligated, to disobey and challenge an instruction that he believed unethical or dangerous to freedom or generally contrary to the spirit of his engagement.

Murder

Murder is the only injury for which no amend or compensation is possible. Nor is it possible for the murderer to be forgiven because the only person with authority to do so is the person murdered. In order to grant the dead the authority that is their due it is not necessary to believe in the immortality of the soul; all that is needed is attention to the fact that as long as a dead person is thought of, and his features, words and actions are remembered, he is still present among the living. To be dead may be to be no more, but it is disastrous to make being dead the same thing as never having been born. When the dead cease to matter, then the living cease to matter too, because any of them can be added to the number of the dead at any time.

What in practice distinguishes an act of power from a rightful act is social reaction to its consummation. If a tort is committed and society fails to obtain reparation, it is as if society did not consider the tort as a tort or the injured person as one of its members. Society has no power to give back a murdered man his life, but if it declines responsibility towards his fate, its institutions cannot be trusted with the safety of any of its members. The antithesis between the factual and the deontological is in no case so sharp and irreducible as in that of murder. According to the fact, he who has been killed is no longer a member of society, while the murderer still is. According to the deontological order, the person killed is still a member of society because he ought to be still alive, while the murderer ought not to be a member of it any longer.

An ethical society does not ascribe to itself the right to punish any of its members but it has a right, and indeed a duty, to preserve its ethicality. If it is powerless to give life back to a murdered man, it has the power to refuse to accept a murderer as one of its members. Thus the sanction of murder is, in an ethical society, loss of social rights. If a murderer still enjoyed them, then murder itself would be accepted as normal and right. If one single person causes one man to die and can still enjoy the society of the living like any other person, then anyone has a right to commit murder and no one can claim the right not to be murdered.

So a murderer will be apprehended and segregated, not as a punishment for what he has done but because society must side with his victim and must maintain its ethical order and the faith that sustains it. Apprehension and segregation are, under modern conditions, the least unethical and yet effective way by which society can separate itself from a murderer and prevent him from reaping any advantages from the death he caused. An ethical society would not prevent a murderer from taking his own life, but it cannot murder a murderer, and eventual restitution of social rights when an alteration of disposition has been shown is not to be excluded.

Part Three **Methods and Means**

Chapter Nine **The Four Ways**

It is not the purpose of this book to examine in detail the steps that might effect the passage from the present to an ideal or anarchist society. The remarks that follow are meant only to provide standards for judgement, certain cautions, perhaps certain challenges, applicable to individual or to concerted and organized actions. Study of methods and means is inseparable from analysis of concrete historical situations. It cannot provide the basis for a successful policy or enter into the making of history without assessment of the organization, alliance, concurrence of wills that at a given time is in search of methods and means. On the other hand, no existing organization and no independent generous impulses can usefully embark upon a course of action without a picture, as honest and clear as possible, of the complexities and dangers – including dangers to the principle of freedom itself – that will be encountered when a trial is made to bring about the conditions necessary for freedom.

If ruthlessness and rigour are to be avoided in practice, principles and ideas will have to be ruthlessly revolutionized and then rigorously adhered to. Anything but the effect intended will be achieved by people who declare themselves partisans of the Rule of Law but refuse to consider honestly the possibility, which we assert to be the case, that the Rule of Law means absence of government. Uncritically identifying absence of government with anarchy in the pejorative sense, they fail to realize that anarchy in that sense is a correct description of any order that is not the ethical order – a correct description, that is, of their own and all other existing or historical societies of any complexity and size.

Ends and means

When dealing with human beings, any distinction between ends and means becomes unethical. It perverts a man's sense of right and wrong, turns well-meaning people into criminals, and, as ends lend themselves to being indefinitely postponed, social injustice becomes a normal and unquestioned practice. The men of today are as important as those of tomorrow and should not be inflicted with evils for the sake of a good that the generation it is meant for may wish to reject. Man and society are ends in themselves, and as all ends come from them, there is none to which they should be sacrificed. To use men as means and to incorporate them in an organization or institution whose purposes transcend them is to turn them into bits of machinery, to degrade them lower than the slaves of antiquity.

The path towards the society of the future can only be ascertained by the present direction of our steps. Nobody knows, nobody has eyes to see, whether after a descent into a valley the path will lead us to higher summits. If we are in darkness and we want to ascend, the sensible thing then is to climb. To go downwards will necessitate retracing our steps later or starting on a new slope that might never take us higher than the point from which we started. He who speaks of lands of innocent happiness just round the corner of a crime, or beyond mountains of crime, is really interested in some immediate effect: to secure and increase his power.

The end does not justify the means, rather, the opposite is true. While ends in fact remain ends, they are simply not present and have no justice with which to justify anything. Means, instead, are actual, they are actions. From their nature and from their immediate results one can judge whether they are just or unjust. If they are just then there is reason to believe that they may be inspired by justice and that justice is their aim. But if they are unjust we do violence to our moral sense and judgement if we believe or even half believe that justice is their aim and inspiration. To judge by ends is to despair of man as a moral being. Ends are beyond verification; to give them authority is to turn them into a God, and to make possible turning any crime into a virtue and any virtue into a crime.

The way of the meek

The renunciation of violence and deception, however motivated, is the first and fundamental condition to the achievement of freedom and peaceful social existence as well as to their preservation once achieved. This renunciation is thus a means-cum-end, a truly moral value.

Whether it is psychologically so embedded as to function effortlessly like a natural habit, or is the result of a moral discipline, renunciation of violence is the mainstay of the ethical capital, and anything that can be called civilized has in it its primary foundation. Thus anyone, anywhere, at any time, makes a contribution towards the ideal society – gives an instance of it on the cellular scale, as it were, while the whole organism remains invisible and unachieved – if his dealings with other men exclude violence, contempt and deception and are based on love, kindness and care. This may be called the way of the meek.

But meekness is not a virtue if practised without attention to the needs of the situation. It is definitely a virtue when practised towards the weak and the dependent, not so definitely when addressed to the powerful and those upon whom one is dependent. Towards the latter meekness serves the interests of self more than the interests of ethics. Meekness is an abiding disposition of harmlessness, an unwillingness and finally an inability to resort to the methods and to stand the strain of violent competition and self-affirmation. Behaviour resembling that of the meek can be used instrumentally for self-protection, but the genuinely meek can be distinguished from the opportunist and the servile in that he is not prompted to cringing adulation, to moral complicity with meekness' contrary, or to contempt for those meeker or weaker than himself. Lack of power alone does not create meekness. The powerless man who is at the mercy of the powerful and is abused by him does not develop meekness in his heart if there is a chance (or if he can dream of a chance) to play the role of the powerful with somebody else. The slave at heart is so abject because by wishing he had the power of his master, and by being ready to behave like his master, he puts himself beyond the redeeming reach of justice and ideals of freedom; and as the victim of a crime that he himself endorses he can hardly be pitied.

Meekness also loses its ethical value when it is the yielding of a person to the will of another who thereby injures a third. If the meek person becomes a weapon in the hands of the violent, no ethical quality abides with him; he is either irresponsible or, if responsible, privy to violence. Peoples and classes subjugated by violence and then made to participate actively in and to endorse publicly the unethical actions of their masters can no longer rely on meekness to live the ethical life.

It is one of the worst features of our time that a man with an ethical disposition may be not only physically but morally a slave to the power of the positive society in which he lives. The question then arises whether he who bows to or carries out the dictates of a wicked will is still a man of good will. Invariably an honest and intelligent analysis of one's implication and entanglement with the cruelties and injustices of the society in which one lives leads either to despair or 'double faith'. Double faith is reliance on two different and opposed systems of values with one's allegiance never given entirely to the one or the other. Both despair and double faith lead to contempt of one's kind and factual indifference, if not hostility, to the ethical issues. They cannot constantly be kept at bay; but honest intelligence and intelligent honesty will not be forsaken if despair and double faith are not once and for all or too often embraced. The exclusion of intellectual honesty from the character equipment by which inner peace or outer efficiency are achieved makes behaviour, judged ethical by inner standards, irretrievably instrumental to injustice and oppression.

Builders and guardians

Because the meek are not only regularly the victims of violence and deception but are also subject to being herded together and constrained to turn themselves into heavy and deadly instruments of multifarious crimes, it is necessary that the ethical capital of the meek be socially registered and guaranteed. It must be witnessed and approved, and defer to that third person usually excluded by ethics of love and other individualistic ethics. An authority must be found, beside or above the changing wills and modes of personal relationships. Whether it be reason or sympathy, the principle of this authority must be concrete and multipersonal, not abstract and impersonal. Thus any social recognition of an ethical way of life, any replacement of naked power by authority, any superseding of frightened and subjugated wills by wills mutually respectful and trustful, any consolidation of freedom in customs and institutions, is a new stone added to the edifice of the ethical society, and this may not inappropriately be called the way of the builders.

Authorities are established by the meek themselves whenever a beneficial or admirable competence appears in their midst. They arise also as a concession by a power that has to rely on the support of the meek in order to bring a battle against another power to a successful conclusion. Following a great social convulsion, they are founded partly in expiation of the faults and mistakes that caused it and partly as a pledge of peace when strife has proved too costly and sterile. However established, no authority is maintained unless the people who exercise it keep alive the spirit that presided over its establishment, and unless they promote the establishment of other authorities by which it will be recognized and which in concert with it will help ensure that the society is ethically founded.

Because the builder's ethical achievements constitute a more tangible and fruitful capital than the sheer availability and malleability of the meek, the partisans of unfairness and exploitation become covetous of them, and unite in strength and shrewdness to make them theirs. As an achievement of authority arises where naked power has been softened or mortified, the achievement stands out as an obvious prey to the exploiters of the ethical capital. If they can capture it without having the air of doing so, if they can disguise their capture under ethical cover or make it soon be forgotten, they will derive from it the spoils of power a hundredfold while expending only a hundredth of the energy and courage needed in brutal assault and looting. Hence the vigilance, the alertness, the incorruptibility and steadfastness required by those invested with authority, whom we may call guardians of the ethical customs and institutions that society has created. The way of the guardians is to denounce any impingement and infringement, to keep naked power at bay, and to pay it back if necessary in its own currency – being wary, however, of introducing this currency for internal use within the sphere of their authority.

Permeation

Seats of authority can be reclaimed from the claws of power by permeating the would-be ethical organizations of the State. The primary condition for 'building' ethical authority under such difficult circumstances is that these organizations be opened to the ethically sound. By systematically stealing anyone who is to occupy a position of power, a totalitarian State aims at making sure that this condition is not realized. But the appeal of a totalitarian State to its cadres must be partly idealistic, and the society from which the cadres are drawn must be kept convinced that the State is serving socially beneficial purposes; power conflicts must be accompanied by concessions to ethics and society if the cadres' faith and society's illusions are not to diminish. As a result the too rigid ideology and discipline of a first generation of totalitarian masters is found inadequate by the next, and the State passes into the hands of men who are less unethical or who rely, from self-interest, on less unethical men. So, for the same reasons and through a similar process as civilized society emerged out of barbarism, seats of authority are reclaimed from totalitarian tyranny. There are limits, in fact, beyond which barbarism and anti-sociality cease to pay.

The resulting tendency is not necessarily constantly favourable, unfortunately. An oscillatory movement has been observed, in one totalitarian State at least, from extremes of oppression to more moderate practices, each reversal being marked by a butchery of scapegoats chosen from those who committed themselves too far to one direction and failed to foresee the impending reversal. But varying degrees of unethicality obtain at different times, and if it is dangerous to show signs of ethicality in a totalitarian State, it is equally dangerous to show too much zeal in oppression. So long as unethicality is not absolute, there are always opportunities for tempering the State's exploitation of the ethical capital.

In a non-totalitarian State, complete subservience is not a necessary condition for participation in government and administration. In the latter, political noncommitment is often an asset. Permeation of the State by ethical elements and use of its organs for the exercise of the rule of authority is partly a reality already, and it would be foolish to disregard the possibilities offered.

Anarchists who think they can help the ethical cause outside the State by taking an open and uncompromising stand against it are certainly right. But the reasons they are so few are more complex than they think, and a necessary condition for any success they achieve is that the State they oppose is tolerant and weak. Such a State is one in which ethical elements are active. Thanks to them, and to the authority of some recognized institution holding its own against power, people persuaded of the unredeemable unethicality of the State can express and publish their opinions practically unmolested. Where the State is strong and determined to establish absolute control over society, open and organized criticism against it is dealt with quickly.

Anti-power

There are areas where authority (that is, the rule of freedom) has been established and is adequately defended by its builders and its guardians. But there are others – whole continents, in fact – where power is entrenched firmly, is hardly affected by permeation, and under heavy or thin disguise carries out its business of oppression and exploitation. Power is by nature imperialistic and aggressive, and no authority is secure from its assaults. The partisans of authority would be constantly on the losing side against those of power but for an inherent superiority of constructiveness of which the latter are jealous and on which they secretly depend, for power is not only outwardly destructive but inwardly sterile. The apparently limitless superiority of power in its instruments of compulsion and suppression should not blind the observer to its congenital weakness – that it becomes more divided internally the stronger it waxes, and is fearful of perishing in the same way as it brought rival powers to an end.

When power is too heavily applied or meets with a too sensitive material, furthermore, it engenders anti-power. Where authority has been obliterated or turned into a mask of power and ethical principles are scarcely even mentioned, when freedom and love have been offended so deeply that human life is no longer humanly livable, then life and humanity rebel. They either offer a silent, death-like resistance in the detachment of despair, or else strike back, perforce unethically and without ethical purpose, and carry out what may be called a scorched-earth policy of the ethical capital, thus robbing power of its purpose and finally defeating it by forcing it to a recall of some authority and peace.

Anti-power is the motive force of genuine revolutions. Being a fruit of desperation, it dissipates as soon as hope returns and, being unethical, it becomes power as soon as it is triumphant. Yet, being different from power in origin and motivation, it is not inconceivable that it could be so disciplined as to defeat power on behalf of authority without itself becoming power. An anti-archist principle, which would embrace any struggle against power that eschewed the exploitive and oppressive methods of power and was deadly and inhuman solely against what has been proven deadly and inhuman, is not only conceivable but possible.

The meek would lie indefinitely and entirely at the mercy of the violent, and authority would be continuously exposed to manoeuvres transforming it into a disguise and instrument of power, if it were not for lessons power learns from anti-power. In realistic terms, the so-called power of authority is the latent anti-power of those who enjoy the rule of freedom that authority ensures; if the authority is vigilant enough, it can muster and fling into action this anti-power whenever it is threatened. Since freedom can always be destroyed by power, wherever there is authority and freedom there must be anti-power, although invisible and unexercised.

The common fate of anti-power, its degeneration into power, is due mainly to its arising in desperate conditions and being exercised by men who have but vague reminiscences of the rule of authority. If ethically rooted and ethically inspired, anti-power can be organized into a struggle to dislodge power from the seats of authority and to dislocate and break down its instruments of oppression and exploitation; then anti-power will not wait for conditions of despair to enter into action, although it will use against power the weapons usually prompted by despair.

As the characteristic feature of anti-power is disciplined courage, we will call its exercise the way of the brave.

At the present, when the need for a worldwide ethical society is so clear and utter catastrophe as the final word of power is a visible prospect, few things serve better the interests of the usurpers of authority and the exploiters of ethical capital than disbelief in the availability and efficacy of anti-power. When it is said that the revolutionary inevitably turns into an oppressor or that any effective political movement must strengthen the State and that the State will not wither away, the ethically inspired are dispirited, and the brave and generous are pushed along the path of corruption and turn upon those who remind them of their formerly uncorrupted self. If historical experience teaches that fighters for freedom may turn into freedom's worst enemies, the sound conclusion is that ever new precautions must be taken to prevent this happening. If States are what they are and do not wither away, then nothing must be done that strengthens them, no opportunity must be lost to weaken parts of their structure; and when States crumble to pieces their restoration or replacement must be stopped.

The revolutionary aftermath

The conditions obtaining on the morrow of the overthrow of an incompetent and oppressive regime are a crucial test of the genuineness and strength of the anti-power credited with the revolutionary victory. Even if genuine and strong anti-power organizations, working together with the masses who wanted and made the revolution, succeed in keeping in check organizations that seek to magnify their own power by allegedly defending the revolution against traitors, reactionaries and saboteurs, such a time is fraught with unethical possibilities.

On the morrow of a revolution a society is not animated exclusively by a will to establish an ethical way of life, even if such a will may be credited with achieving the social unity necessary for the success of the revolution. A revolution is not a purgative of which the social organism relieves itself along with the decaying and toxic material that made the revolution necessary. Apart from feuds between organizations and gangs that took part in the revolution and are ready to sacrifice its purpose and achievements to self-aggrandizement, there are people and classes in no way disposed to act in a spirit of social good will and constructive cooperation. People who held positions of privilege and command before the revolution are justifiably resentful if their removal overstepped the limits of fairness and was vicious and insulting. There are people who fought for the old regime because they identified it with society and saw its opponents as an incarnation of evil, and even if they should recognize that they fought for the wrong cause they will not readily forget the violence suffered by themselves or their relatives and friends. Others, some of them partisans of the old regime and some not, suffered violence from revolutionaries who in the absence of any rule of authority took liberties with property and persons and relied on an impunity they believed to be their due. On the other hand, those who suffered exploitation under the old regime, or violence from its supporters, will consider it the first duty of justice to satisfy their thirst for vengeance.

To these difficulties must be added the hampering and frustrating activities of people without competence of ability or interest who achieve positions of authority because authority had to be wrenched from the hands of power and they happened to be the men who did the wrenching. They are loath to give up their positions. Even more recalcitrant are those who enjoyed the violence and licence of anti-power conditions and, by exaggerating and occasionally concocting power conspiracies and counter-attacks, hope to persuade others and themselves that anti-power still has an important part to play.

To the social disunity we have outlined must be added the fact, of capital importance for the integral pacifist, that violence begets more violence. Unfortunately both for the integral pacifist and for mankind, when the violent and non-violent come to a clash of wills the violent is more likely to have his way. The organizers and leaders of an anti-power struggle become its exploiters because their experience leads them to believe in the efficacy of violence. They do not attempt to unravel the Gordian knot of wrongs and hatreds in which society is enmeshed. Their solution is to eliminate all those who, having been harmed or wronged by the revolution, have reasons to hamper its course. Once elimination has been decided upon, the high percentage of people to which it is applied does not cause the decision to be abandoned.

Elimination if carried out thoroughly will give society the unity it lacked. There should remain only the ardent supporters of the revolution and those who, knowing no better, can be made to believe that it is the best of possible worlds. The submission of reason to the *fait accompli* of elimination rests on such evidence as that nobody really worries today about the Red Indians or the Tasmanian aborigines, and that worrying would not help them in any way. On the other hand, physical elimination of these races has not destroyed their historical presence. Without their record of bloody conquest and exploitation, the Western nations would not be so hated by Africans and Asiatics, and many people might be ready to fight and fight more willingly for the democracy that Western nations claim to be inspired by. There is evidence of historical guilt – of racial, national and class guilt – and the conception of historical nemesis is not to be dismissed.

The fact is that the method of elimination does not achieve social unity or help institutions born of the revolution to be ethically based. Even supposing it never errs in the choice of its victims, it requires that the whole of society be at the mercy of the eliminating power. This power waxes and concentrates in the hands of specialists without social sense or respect for the human person and without care for the ethical capital. To retain power, they confuse all ethical issues and lay the system that arose from the revolution open to the same condemnation as was pronounced on the one destroyed. In the long run, as intelligence and ethical will are insuppressible, a social condemnation gathers over the eliminators, even if they are still busy at their job after forty or fifty years. Their claim to represent anti-power is no longer believed; the need of a rule of authority and the emergence of new anti-power spell their end and will eventually bring it about.

Another solution to the tangled problems arising from the violent overthrow of an oppressive regime is a general amnesty and a spirit of forgiveness. Unfortunately, forgiveness cannot be ordered, and if it should be suggested on the morrow of a revolution the obvious retort would be that no revolution should then have been made. Also, if past crimes are going to be forgiven and escape retribution, any further crime that may still be committed should be forgiven likewise.

Violent overthrow of power may be a prelude to conditions favourable to ethical life only if victorious anti-power makes room immediately for the rule of authority, stands by as its guardian as long as needed, and does not usurp its functions or exert such pressure on authority's organs as would transform them into instruments of tyranny. Ethical principles must be applied straightaway, and the organizational forms of anarchist society must be embodied as soon as, and whenever, competence of ability is available. The armed forces of the revolution should be reduced to the role of emergency corps, their main duty being to contain any fresh outburst of violence, to see that judicial decisions are carried out, to protect these authorities from intimidation, and to prevent evasion or usurpation of their functions. Cultural authorities, which should immediately replace armed formations and be given the freedom that is theirs in an anarchist society, can help the judiciary greatly by assuming collective responsibility for wrongs and reparations and by solving conflicts through the creation of intercultural authorities.

Concerning the wrong of murder, for which there is no reparation, assessors responsible for application of justice will find themselves in a particularly delicate position, since hardly any leading exponent of the revolutionary forces will be without at least one death on his conscience. If discriminations were made between those who fought for the revolution and those who fought against it, there would be no justice in the ethical sense. Murder is always murder, whoever the victim, and responsibility for murder lies with a person issuing an order to kill as with the actual killer. Killing in self-defence is the only case in which the killer need not lose the trust of his fellow beings. Both partisans of power and partisans of anti-power who killed people who were out to kill them must be considered as having killed in self-defence. If, however, they killed unarmed persons, persons who had been or could have been safely captured and disarmed, hostages, persons who were just in the way, or persons who they could not be bothered to ascertain were enemies or not, then self-defence cannot be alleged. The claim of self-defence will be accepted, instead, if the dead person is ascertained to have been a killer or to have ordered others to kill.

The main and final object of anti-power is to remove from society all persons who have power to order others to kill. No authority is safe while such power is unassailable or legalized. Care for anything social becomes of dubious value while society admits people whose function is to give orders to kill and others whose duty is to obey those orders. The sign by which anti-power will be recognized as genuine is its concentration on excluding persons and organizations that make ethical life impossible. The guarantee that anti-power will withdraw in the hour of its triumph to make room for the rule of authority will lie in its having carried out its revolutionary struggle with no homicide committed except under a valid and truthful circumstance of self-defence.

Chapter Ten The Anti-Power Struggle

While rebellion remains the only way of shaking off power to make room for authority, it is clear from what has been said that revolution is undesirable. Though it is not to be opposed when it comes as generalized rebellion, it must not be deliberately sought. Its ravages equal or surpass the ravages of war, and the phase of decentralization of power it goes through – which for some people is all that anarchy means – leads finally to a new centralization in many ways more tyrannical than the old.

Leninist theory and practice have made it an axiom, among all the have-nots of power, masses and would-be leaders alike, that every oppressive political and economic system is based on force and can only be overthrown by force. Any reform or improvement by pacific means is looked upon with suspicion and contempt as a ruse or a sign of weakness on the part of the privileged. Force, sometimes of the most ruthless and vicious kind, is indeed what most systems finally rest on, but the same is true of those who are organizing for their overthrow.

Is there a way out of the dilemma whereby rebellion must be renounced for the sake of ethics or ethics for the sake of rebellion? We believe that there is. While fighting against power with one hand, the anarchist must protect society with the other. While concomitant, the two tasks are far from being identical and, from the principle that there must be only one set of standards and one vocabulary, the anarchist must let his right hand know what his left is doing. Rebellion there must be wherever there is power. The many awaiting salvation through revolution or overthrow of a State must be shown that any organization preparing for the seizure of power is as reactionary as any that already holds it, and that it is itself but a State. It is already exercising a will to rule the masses, not to free them. As rival powers are eliminated, its rule will be, if not harsher, more complete.

As long as there is power, we repeat, there must be rebellion, but rebellion against incipient forms of power as well as against those established. That movement and those organizations will show themselves truly anarchist that will not practise, and will not structure themselves according to, the very methods they condemn in others. Power is power under any name. A revolutionary power, wanting the end of one system of oppression, is no guarantee against itself embodying another such system. That it is but another system of oppression can be seen by the way it deals with any body of men who, though clearly no friends of the former oppressors, are treated as if they were simply because they represent an independent seat of authority and power.

When not directly involved, it is easy to deny that there is any difference between power and anti-power. When one is directly involved, eagerness for the struggle and its outcome only too easily makes one dismiss ethical considerations that, honestly acknowledged, might lead one to retrace one's steps and to undo things already done, and this requires far more courage than marching straight ahead. Yet there are ways of detecting power methods and power directions in anti-power movements even before they have come to power.

If within an anti-power movement, for example, the principle of leadership obtains against the principle of authority in any department but that of direct struggle against power, then the first gains of some well-meaning fighters for freedom are being made instrumental to the establishment of a new tyranny. So also if the strength of will or the weapons or the material means of an anti-power organization are used against the meek; or if instances of oppression and exploitation occur within the movement and criticism thereof is violently resented; or if centralization exercises its lure and its apostles are quite clear about who will be at the centre; or if sophistry, tergiversation or actual violence are used to prevent or delay the installation or restoration of authority when there is opportunity for it; then, in all these cases, anti-power is being contaminated and there are forces at work threatening to turn it, from within, into a duplication of power. If the anti-power will is there, however, and if it has been duly tempered and enlightened, there should be no lack of intelligence to read these signs and no lack of determination to use whatever courage can be spared to stop the incipient rot in time.

To renounce or despair of the anti-power struggle is to accept injustice and oppression as normal and final. The anti-power struggle is renounced not so much when specifically anti-power organizations are lacking as when nothing is done to denounce, prevent and hinder the misdeeds and the hypocrisies of power – when, that is, thought ceases to be alerted by human sympathies and to be engaged in finding means to avert and relieve man-made suffering. Regardless of the inner perfection and harmony that can conceivably be achieved by such renunciation, the ethical cause is as good as abandoned.

One must not be blind to the great and fundamental difference between disinterestedness and all-interestedness, even though their manifestations sometimes agree. In all-interestedness lies the full assertion of man's responsibility to hunt and defeat evil. To renounce evil and to make oneself more or less invulnerable to it is a great achievement, but it is only half a moral achievement if evil is given a free hand against others who have not the means, the leisure or the grace to make themselves equally invulnerable and whom evil will either crush or enrol in its service. The ideal solution is, of course, that those who exercise power or benefit from it should recognize it as evil and lay it down. But without denunciation and opposition from those they fleece and tread upon, without any expression of dignity and courage from below, they are bound to consider their power as proof of human excellence, and to regard those they oppress as subhuman and deserving to be used, abused, and coolly or thrillingly crushed.

The renunciation of power by those who hold it is not to be exclusively or even preponderantly counted upon, but neither is it to be disparaged or discounted. Voluntary surrender of privileges and the passing of some of the privileged to the opposing camp have proved on many occasions to be important, even decisive, in both revolution and reform. A renunciation of power that automatically results in the taking up of that power by another is not so much to be hoped for and encouraged as is the transformation of power into authority in normal times, or into anti-power in times ripe for an open struggle.

As power in its present structures has to disguise itself as authority practically everywhere, it is possible practically everywhere to frustrate power by making the disguise operate as reality. This requires courage and shrewdness, and it requires men who, if not prepared to sacrifice personal safety, are prepared to sacrifice at least a career and not a few of the advantages of the measure of power with which they are entrusted.

The breaking up of power from within by restoration of authority can be the result of isolated individual endeavours, but in a police State it would have to be both discreet and well organized. There is indeed more than one analogy, regarding the relationship of power to the ethical ideal, between our time and the eighteenth century – the century of flourishing secret societies as well as of enlightenment. The clandestine organizations of our time, however, should and could – despite the conditions forced upon them by police, party and other species of totalitarian State – organize themselves on anti-power lines; that is, not in blind obedience but in a spirit of vigilance and self-respect on the part of all members. They should rely on decentralized though concomitant leadership, have no recourse to the power method of compulsion within their organization, and in the exercise of anti-power they should aim at restoring positions of command to authority rather than at capturing such positions. That is, such organizations should never secure any power or allow any member to do so, except in order to break down more power. Finally and above all they should consider as no longer a member, but as an enemy, anyone who breaks down authority or abuses the meek.

The role of religions

Most religions and most cultural systems support the ethical
effort with a transcendent imperative and justification, with
a mystical collective sanction, and with a ritual that regularly feeds the persuasions of faith. They are also often the
originators of ethical efforts, and those who live under their
inspiration believe that without the religion or cultural
system there would be no ethics. They have proved in-
valuable if not indispensable to the framing of ethical principles and to the definition and establishment of modes of
ethical behaviour, although some of them profess to make
little of the world where the ethical society awaits its realization.

Although religions may postulate an original sin or give it
as axiomatic that there is a gap in the texture of man and
Nature, the evidence is overwhelming that salvation, peace
of mind, relief from guilt or whatever religions consider
man's supreme task or *unum necessarium*, supports ethical
behaviour and does not offend it. Religions have, however,
proved repeatedly to be, and can still constitute, an obstacle
of the first magnitude to peaceful living and respect for the
human person, either because these two values are not included in their set of values or because the realization of
some other value is taught by their devotees as worth securing at the expense of peace and by means of torture, death
and the infliction of indignities on the human person.

Men of piety, of deep reflection, of inner peace, chari-
tableness and detachment, are already citizens of the anarchist society. It is primarily by an increasing number of
people whose actions have bestowed upon them the right of
this citizenship that the city itself will be realized. Political
organizations tend to enforce alienation of conscience, to
measure man according to his usability, and to make power
absolute. Before wishing for or working for the disappearance of any religion, it is well to ask which political
organization will profit from it, and to remember that a Lord
in heaven can always be appealed to against the lords of the
earth, that belief in the eternal softens the tyranny of the

temporal, and that people with a religious faith have proven to be not the last in resisting the establishment and excesses of a totalitarian rule.

The meek, in fact, must not be thought to be devoid of strength or unable to use it. It is from them, when tried beyond endurance, that comes the force of despair that acts as genuine anti-power. Under normal circumstances, however, their strength is faith – faith in Someone or Something stronger than themselves and stronger than all the power that delights in stamping on their faces. They know against all apparent evidence that this Someone or Something is on their side and not on that of power. It is consciously and not without effort that they often persevere in meekness so as to be sure that they keep on the side of this Someone or Something above all power, and so that there be even in this world a token of something clean and worthy of the beyond. This faith is often described and dismissed as the result of simple-mindedness and poverty of spirit, yet its conclusions are found amazingly to coincide with those suggested by some of mankind's greatest thinkers. It is itself a form of intelligence, and it certainly serves the higher purposes to which intelligence can be put. Far from being the people's opiate, it dries up at the sources, or persuades to the rejection of, that which whether sold under a religious or irreligious label is the people's worst poison.

Modern religions, as contrasted with tribal religions, are almost exclusively associations of the meek. But their authorities as a rule are only nominally concerned with the authority of the Someone or Something above all power, while they are accepted as useful mediators both by the powerful and the meek. They serve the meek in restraining power, and serve the powerful by preventing meekness from being turned into anti-power; and while doing their job competently, they draw not a few advantages from both parties.

The mass of the meek can do a tremendous service to the ethical cause by relying more on faith and less on its interpretations, by vigilantly living up to the antithesis be-

tween the Someone or Something of their faith and the
worldly powers, and finally by severing their associations
from links of subordination and loyalty to the latter. It so
happens that the purposes of inwardness and those of the
ethical cause coincide or, at least, are not mutually hostile.
Any stress upon inwardness within the associations of the
meek is therefore a victory for the ethical cause. Within
these associations, there can be deliberately fostered what we
may call a process of anarchization – that is, affirmation of
the competence of interest and ability against any en-
croachment and disguise of power. For in the spiritual
matters on which these associations claim to be founded,
competence of interest pertains only to God and the individual soul, and competence of ability is the competence of
the saint, not that which is claimed by the priest on grounds
against which intelligence, inwardness and ethicality
rebel.

Decentralization, mistrust of the principle of leadership
and spiritual autonomy are achievements that, secured
within the associations of the meek, will not fail greatly to
facilitate the ethical cause and to gain finer conditions for
the furthering of the spiritual life that is their principal
interest. Contrary to the assumption and policies of most
Church authorities, conditions of the greatest religious and
individual freedom – which it is the purpose of an ethical
society to establish – and not of greatest material welfare or
of maximum power, will afford the best opportunities for
what they believe to be their founders' vital message and for
man's spiritual quest.

Moral hubris

The failure of many honest and heroic attempts to re-
generate society is due to internal weakness and degeneration, and if this internal cancer could be detected and
removed the chances of external power dealing them the
mortal blow would be greatly diminished. Unfortunately, as
with cancers that attack living organisms, this cause of revolutionary degeneration seems connatural with the body it

attacks; so much so that, although its ill effects are frequently noticed, it has not been isolated, given a name, or described in a detail that would permit its symptoms to be easily recognized and surgical intervention to occur. Even assuming that it is in no way pathological but part and parcel of human nature there is no reason for being fatalistically resigned to its having its way, because ethical inspiration is equally part and parcel of human nature and one must swallow or get rid of the other. This condition is a form and mixture of archism, self-interest, pride and ambition. Itself a product of confusion, it thrives on confusion, and so an attempt will be made here to describe it with accuracy. To it will be given the name that seems to us most apposite, 'moral hubris'.

Moral hubris manifests itself at first as a particularly robust and rapidly growing will to achieve an ethical purpose. But soon a critical and diagnostically important time comes when the subject affected with moral hubris most determinedly decides that what matters is, not that the ethical purpose be achieved, but that *he* be the primary or supreme achiever. The more genuine the devotion to an ethical purpose, and the more he has given tangible signs of it and brought it within sight of final achievement, the more difficult it becomes for him to see himself separate from all that is ethical and to imagine that others see him separate from it in their minds.

So when some who are at his side or follow in his wake show signs of hostility to him, or appear to doubt the honesty and purity of his intentions, the moral hubrist will see in those men hypocrites or traitors. He will also hate them violently because he will see in them the reflection greatly magnified of his own hubris, without the ethicality of achievement by which he sees himself redeemed. Even more will he hate those who are fighting with better fortune and are more likely to achieve that very ethical purpose that he has grown to consider his right. It is with these feelings and under these circumstances that competence of ability is claimed by a person or group against another, and that in the absence of competence of recognition the principle of authority is forgone and trampled upon in order firmly to establish the principle of leadership.

Rivalry between two movements claiming to be inspired by similar ethical purposes, and both more or less directed against the same power, may give rise to the danger of moral hubris. It will be a mark of the ethicality of the movements if they can be brought together to solve their rivalry by peaceful and equitable means. Their failure to do so would be a sign for their adherents that moral hubris has already warped the movement or organization, and that either or both are already contaminated by power, or that they stand to each other in the unethical relation of rival powers though both still stand as anti-power in respect to a third. They should negotiate and come to agreement delimiting the sphere of their respective authorities in terms of competence of interest as represented by actual members and areas of operation, and of competence of ability as represented by verifiable achievements. Any attempt at fusion at the top or at the centre is to be regarded as a power manoeuvre, while cooperation and even fusion is instead to be encouraged locally on an autonomous and decentralized scale.

When the danger of moral hubris is internal to the organization (taking for instance the form of rivalry between old and new blood) one solution could be divided leadership or the amicable split of the organization. Much preferable would be the creation or mediation of authority in a third person, not committed to either side. The decision of this impartial authority, or of one consisting of supporters of both sides, determined however to avoid the dangers of moral hubris at all costs, should be to the effect of demanding some sacrifice of leadership and authority from both rivals, especially if their competence of ability can safely be replaced.

Solidarity of the ethically inspired

Most important of all, and the real clue to the success of a struggle with ethical aims, is the determined practical application of the following principle: no person, movement or organization can qualify as ethically competent if part of its work is deliberately to hamper or frustrate the ethical competence or endeavour of other persons, movements or organizations. The rule of authority and respect for freedom has to be applied here and now, at every start and step towards an anarchist society. The use of anti-power is justified only against power. Against anything else it is anti-power no longer, but power, and of the most insidious kind when used to defame or supplant what it is itself no longer. A movement with monopolistic or imperialistic tendencies can lay no claim to being ethical, however much it may recommend itself on other grounds.

More specifically, ethicality is not achieved, but only the cause of power served, when there is no practical recognition of the legitimacy and necessity of all four ways: of the meek, of the builders, of the guardians and of the brave. No one – genius or not – and no science or history, have the right to decide which way is the right way for any person at any time. Endorsement of this right, on the other hand, whether as a rule or an exception, means endorsement of the right to enforce decisions, and is one with power believed in and practised.

The four ways are complementary to one another, and the success of the ethical cause depends on reciprocal tolerance and solidarity among their respective choosers. The implementation of this solidarity of the four ways will be at the same time the implementation of the principles stressed at the beginning of this Part, that separation of ends and means is characteristically unethical and, as corollary, that anti-power is legitimate on biological rather than on ethical grounds.

There frequently occur among fighters for the same worthy cause bitter internal struggles that are not due to moral hubris. A careful study of their causes, patterns of development and results would provide those determined to preserve the conditions necessary to the integrity and success of an ethical cause with means of forestalling and nipping them in the bud. It seems likely that the sacrifices a difficult cause demands induce a mood of masochism and exasperation, or perhaps an expiatory goat is obscurely felt to be necessary to ally temporary impotence, slowness and awkwardness in achievement. It is all too true that more energies are thus wasted in internecine struggles between members of the same group, or between movements closely allied in composition, purpose and appeal, than are used by them separately or conjointly against their supposedly common enemy.

The ostensible intent of these struggles is usually unity of leadership, but since leadership even at its purest is unethical the merger aimed at by such wasteful and even dangerous struggles must constantly be opposed; and if the necessity of unity for the sake of efficiency is invoked, let there be unity of purpose but diversity of action, or unity of action with safeguarded variety of purpose. A movement is lost to all ethical purposes when transformed into a party machine, and coordinated action must never be confused with unity of leadership. On the other hand, although the evils of leadership and power may infiltrate any organization, their denunciation may be just an instrument in the hands of rival evils of the same kind. Whether the denunciation springs from ethical interests or not can be tested by asking the question *'Cui bono?'*, by analysing the measures proposed or implicit in the denunciation and by foreseeing the logical results of their implementation.

An anarchist society, if ever realized, will be realized universally. But any immediate attempt to create a worldwide organization for the specific purpose of achieving this society would be like building a house starting from the roof, and would defeat its purpose because it would claim a competence of interest that is has not. It would be, in other words, usurping authority, adding or superimposing itself upon already organized ethical endeavours. Its fate would be very much like that of an artificially created international language, soon rivalled by others equally artificial, and none of them succeeding in supplanting any of their natural predecessors unless it be by compulsion. It is recognition and not absorption and centralization of authority that will achieve the anarchist society.

Something of the anarchist society is achieved in every instance in which a person or an organization meets with the respect of other organizations and persons. Faith in ethical success, and ethical success itself, are nourished not by organizations straining to affirm and extend their claim to ethicality but by their being neighboured, and credited with ethicality, by other ethical organizations. The ethically committed will recognize their friends by their works, by seeing those friends working for the same cause, and by being ethically treated by them; not by having their intelligence paralysed by the same slogans, by wearing the same badge or being able to produce the same membership card.

Index